CREATING A WORLD THAT WORKS FOR ALL

SHARIF ABDULLAH

Introductory Essay by Václav Havel

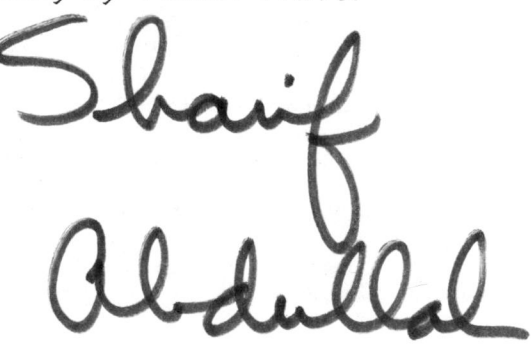

 Berrett-Koehler Publishers, Inc.
San Francisco

Berrett-Koehler Publishers, Inc.
450 Sansome Street, Suite 1200
San Francisco, CA 94111-3320
Tel: (415) 288-0260   Fax: (415)362-2512   www.bkconnection.com

ORDERING INFORMATION

Quantity sales. Special discounts are available on quantity purchases by corporations, associations, and others. For details, contact the "Special Sales Department" at the Berrett-Koehler address above.

Individual sales. Berrett-Koehler publications are available through most bookstores. They can also be ordered direct from Berrett-Koehler: Tel: (800) 929-2929; Fax: (802) 864-7626; www.bkconnection.com

Orders for college textbook/course adoption use. Please contact Berrett-Koehler: Tel: (800) 929-2929; Fax: (802) 864-7626.

Orders by U.S. trade bookstores and wholesalers. Please contact Publishers Group West, 1700 Fourth Street, Berkeley, CA 94710. Tel: (510) 528-1444; Fax (510) 528-3444.

Printed in the United States of America

Printed on acid-free and recycled paper that is composed of 50% recovered fiber, including 10% post consumer waste).

Library of Congress Cataloging-in-Publication Data
Abdullah, Sharif M.
   Creating a world that works for all / Sharif Abdullah. — 1st ed.
     p. cm.
   Includes bibliographical references and index.
   ISBN 1-57675-062-0 (alk. paper)
   1. Conduct of life. 2. Social change. I. Title.
BJ1595.A23 1999
170'.44—dc21
                                           99-29159
                                           CIP

First Edition

05   04   03   02   01   00   99   10 9 8 7 6 5 4 3 2 1

Interior design and composition by Beverly Butterfield, Girl of the West Productions

To my mother, who loved me as she knew how,
and didn't do too bad a job with me.

And to my father, who perhaps one day
will discover that what he thought was a problem
was really an opportunity.

CONTENTS

Note by Sharif Abdullah:

When I started thinking about who might provide an introduction to this book, only one person came to mind. Václav Havel's writing has been such an influence on me, both personally and professionally, that he was the indisputable choice.

Havel stands apart from all other influences. It's one thing to talk about revolution; Havel actually catalyzed one. It's one thing to talk about values; it's quite another to apply those values, from a position of responsibility and leadership, in the world of the mundane and the practical. Havel has elevated the phrase "walk the talk" to the level of national and international politics.

I believe President Havel has written some of the most important political analysis of the past 250 years. Not since Thomas Jefferson has a political figure presented with such power and clarity the need for a new way of doing politics.

I believe the following essay is Havel's clearest statement of the philosophy embodied in the "Velvet Revolution." I remember first reading it in my favorite coffeehouse, smiling at every paragraph. Even before I had finished it, I knew it would be perfect as the introduction to this book.

In this essay, we find not only Havel's deep understanding of our current global predicament but also his crucial insight that the solution lies in a new set of planetary values rooted in the realm of the Spirit.

My thanks to Havel for being a major guiding light in the movement for a world that works for all and for granting me permission to use his essay as an overture to this book.

INTRODUCTORY ESSAY

VÁCLAV HAVEL
President of the Czech Republic

HUMANKIND TODAY IS WELL AWARE of the spectrum of threats looming over its head. We know that the number of people living on our planet is growing at a soaring rate and that within a relatively short time we can expect it to total in the tens of billions. We know that the already-deep abyss separating the planet's poor and rich could deepen further, and more and more dangerously, because of this rapid population growth. We also know that we've been destroying the environment on which our existence depends and that we are headed for disaster by producing weapons of mass destruction and allowing them to proliferate.

And yet, even though we are aware of these dangers, we do almost nothing to avert them. It's fascinating to me how preoccupied people are today with catastrophic prognoses, how books containing evidence of impending crises become bestsellers, but how little account we take of these threats in our everyday activities. Doesn't every schoolchild know that the resources of this planet are limited and that if they are expended faster than they are recovered, we are doomed? And still we continue in our wasteful ways and don't even seem perturbed. Quite the contrary: Rising production is considered to be the main sign of national success, not only in poor states where such a position could be justified, but also in wealthy ones, which are cutting the branch on which they sit with their ideology of indefinitely prolonged and senseless growth.

The most important thing we can do today is to study the reasons why humankind does little to address these threats and why it allows itself to be carried onward by some kind of perpetual motion, unaffected by self-awareness or a sense of future options. It would be unfair to ignore the existence of numerous projects for averting these dangers, or to deny that a lot already has been done. However, all attempts of this kind have one thing in common: They do not touch the seed from which the threats I'm speaking of sprout, but merely try to diminish their impact. (A typical example is the list of legal acts, ordinances, and international treaties stipulating how much toxic matter this or that plant may discharge into the environment.) I'm not criticizing these safeguards; I'm only saying that they are technical tricks that have no real effect on the substance of the matter.

What, then, is the substance of the matter? What could change the direction of today's civilization?

It is my deep conviction that the only option is a change in the sphere of the spirit, in the sphere of human conscience. It's not enough to invent new machines, new regulations, new institutions. We must develop a new understanding of the true purpose of our existence on earth. Only by making such a fundamental shift will we be able to create new models of behavior and a new set of values for the planet. In short, it appears to me that it would be better to start from the head rather than the tail.

Whenever I've gotten involved in a major global problem—the logging of rainforests, ethnic or religious intolerance, the brutal destruction of indigenous cultures—I've always discovered somewhere in the long chain of events that gave rise to it a basic lack of responsibility for the planet.

There are countless types of responsibility—more or less pressing, depending on who's involved. We feel responsible for our personal welfare, our families, our companies, our communities, our nations. And somewhere in the background there is, in every one of us, a small feeling of responsibility for the planet and its future. It seems to me that this last and deepest responsibility has become a very low priority—dangerously low, considering that the world today is more interlinked than ever before and that we are, for all intents and purposes, living one global destiny.

At the same time, our world is dominated by several great religious systems, whose differences seem to be coming to the fore with increasing sharpness and setting the stage for innumerable political and armed conflicts. In my opinion, this fact—which is attracting, understandably, a great deal of media attention—partly conceals a more important fact: that the civilization within which this religious tension is taking place is, in essence, a deeply atheistic one. Indeed, it is the first atheistic civilization in the history of humankind.

Perhaps the real issue is a crisis of respect for the moral order extended to us from above, or simply a crisis of respect for any kind of authority higher than our own earthly being, with its material and thoroughly ephemeral interests. Perhaps our lack of responsibility for the planet is only the logical consequence of the modern conception of the universe as a complex of phenomena controlled by certain scientifically identifiable laws, formulated for God-knows-what purpose. This is a conception that does not inquire into the meaning of existence and renounces any kind of metaphysics, including its own metaphysical roots.

In the process, we've lost our certainty that the universe, nature, existence, our own lives are works of creation that have a definite meaning and purpose. This loss is accompanied by loss of the feeling that whatever we do must be seen in the light of a higher order of which we are part and whose authority we must respect.

In recent years the great religions have been playing an increasingly important role in global politics. Since the fall of communism, the world has become multipolar instead of bipolar, and many countries outside the hitherto dominant Euro-American cultural sphere have grown in self-confidence and influence. But the more closely tied we are by the bonds of a single global civilization, the more the various religious groups emphasize all the ways in which they differ from each other. This is an epoch of accentuated spiritual, religious, and cultural "otherness."

How can we restore in the human mind a shared attitude to what is above if people everywhere feel the need to stress their otherness? Is there any sense in trying to turn the human mind to the heavens when such a turn would only aggravate the conflict among our various deities?

I'm not, of course, an expert of religion, but it seems to me that the major faiths have much more in common than they are willing to admit. They share a basic point of departure—that this world and our existence are not freaks of chance but rather part of a mysterious, yet integral, act whose sources, direction, and purpose are difficult for us to perceive in their entirety. And they share a large complex of moral imperatives that this mysterious act implies. In my view, whatever differences these religions might have are not as important as these fundamental similarities.

Perhaps the way out of our current bleak situation could be found by searching for what unites the various religions—a purposeful search for common principles. Then we could cultivate human coexistence while, at the same time, cultivating the planet on which we live, suffusing it with the spirit of this religious and ethical common ground—what I would call the common spiritual and moral minimum.

Could this be a way to stop the blind perpetual motion dragging us toward hell? Can the persuasive words of the wise be enough to achieve what must be done? Or will it take an unprecedented disaster to provoke this kind of existential revolution—a universal recovery of the human spirit and renewed responsibility for the world?[1]

PREFACE

W E ARE IN DEEP TROUBLE. We live in a world that works for only a few. As for the rest of us, we live in an insecure world, a world threatened by violence, lack, and spiritual malaise. We live one paycheck, one crop, one relationship away from disaster. We may be threatened by men with guns who invade our communities and our peace with threats of violence. Ethnic hatred, from Los Angeles to Djakarta, from Russia to South Africa, threatens our way of life. The world doesn't even work for the materially privileged. Increasing uncertainty, family violence, cancer, a polluted environment, and a diminished outlook for all of the world's children cloud the future for us all.

However, in the midst of this unprecedented disharmony, we have an opportunity that may not come again for another millennium: to craft a society that actually reflects our deepest values. In a world seemingly going in a million directions at once, we can, and must, choose a direction, a focus, an intention. At no other time has it been so clear: our future is our choice.

Our grandchildren will look back at this moment and marvel at the courage, foresight, and plain common sense we demonstrated in pulling ourselves back from the brink of global collapse. Instead of cursing us for our selfishness and shortsightedness, it is my hope that they will offer us their blessings. *Creating a World That Works for All* is my gift to them—a testament of hope.

For me, writing this book has been, paradoxically, both an act of supreme arrogance and an act of deep humility. The arrogance lies in the audacious belief that I have something to say. The humility comes from the realization that none of this is "mine." The knowledge, learning, analysis, and experience that have gone into this book do not belong to me; if anything, I belong to the book, and all of the other books by all of the other authors who have encouraged us to be better than we are. In the words of the Sufi mystic Jelaluddin Rumi,

> *Do you think I know what I'm doing?*
> *That for one breath or half-breath I belong to myself?*
> *As much as a pen knows what it's writing*
> *or the ball can guess where it's going next.*[2]

Rumi talks about the contrasting qualities of a stone and a jewel. The stone blocks light, a jewel transmits it, shaping and coloring it but knowing that the Source of the light lies elsewhere. Arrogance is the stonelike belief that "I" wrote this book. Humility is recognizing that "my" ideas actually come from elsewhere. I hope to be clear enough for the light to shine through.

The life experiences that have prepared me for this project are not ones that I chose. I did not ask for poverty, welfare, an emotionally distant mother and a nonexistent father. I did not ask for my teenage years to be filled with sadistically racist cops and a school system ranked as the worst in the nation. Had I been in control of my circumstances, I would have programmed a happier beginning—and middle.

Humility comes, in part, from realizing that my nightmare upbringing—worse than some, not as bad as others—served as the catalyst for this book. Everything in life conspires to bring each of us to this moment in time, with this consciousness and these understandings. If our painful experiences are to have any meaning in the world, it is to shine a light on all those things that desperately need to be changed.

In May of 1998, as I stood in the ruins of one of the killing factories at Auschwitz, surrounded by fields of daisies fertilized with the ashes of the slaughtered, my thoughts went to other killing fields, in Bosnia, Rwanda, Cambodia, Vietnam . . . If we are to honor the slain of Auschwitz and every other site of barbarous inhumanity, we must create the consciousness that makes such slaughter impossible.

The past is our teacher. The proof that we have learned its lessons will come when our present horrors become unthinkable in our time. Obviously, we have much to learn.

Appreciations and Acknowledgments

The Spiritual Ground
My spiritual house rests on four pillars: Rumi, Jesus, Buddha, and Lao Tzu. For thousands of years, they have been teaching us that the world can work for all.

The Students of Inclusivity
To all of the students, interns, workshop participants, trainees, and others who think they learned something from me. Most of what I know was learned from them.

Places of the Heart
Many times, a place can have as profound an influence on the direction of my work as a person. This book has been shaped by the places in which it was written, including the Sylvia Beach Hotel in Newport, Oregon; Bar Montserrate in Havana, Cuba (down the street from Ernest Hemingway's watering hole, the Floridita); and the Globe Bookstore in Prague.

Editors, Readers, and Reviewers

Steve Piersanti and Stanley Marcus, for displaying editorial valor above and beyond the call of duty. This book, in its present form, exists largely because of their continued patient editorial assistance. Over the years, Steve helped shape "a collection of profound ideas" into a book. And Stanley's copyediting skills helped to make the book logical, internally consistent, and readable.

David Sweet, for key editorial assistance at a crucial juncture, as well as for being a fountain of quotable quotes. Chisao Hata, for reviewing from the right side of the brain. Scott Sherman, for his help with early manuscripts. Other reviewers include Gar Alperovitz, Kim Kelley, David and Fran Korten, Paul Niebanck, Gifford and Libba Pinchot, Richard Seidman, Brian Setzler, and Sarah Van Gelder.

Thanks to the reviewers commissioned by Berrett-Koehler and to the staff at Berrett-Koehler for additional value-added editorial assistance.

Personal Support

To Chisao, for being there consistently through thick and thin, through twenty-plus edits, high points, low points, psychotic episodes, moments of joy, delusions of grandeur, and delusions of minisculeur.

SHARIF ABDULLAH
Portland, Oregon
April 1999

INTRODUCTION

A CENTURY AGO, coal miners carried canaries down into the depths of the mines. The miners did not take their canaries into the mines because they thought they were beautiful. They did not keep canaries as pets. The canaries were present for only one purpose: to warn the miners of the poisonous but odorless gases that could asphyxiate without warning. The canary was there as an early warning system; if it died, the miners would abandon their work pronto, because they knew they were next. Their fate was inextricably linked to that of a small songbird.

Today, we live in a society littered with the bodies of dead canaries. There are ever mounting statistics, from a variety of sources, warning us that our social, ecological, even spiritual lives are out of balance. But few are paying attention. We do not see the relationships between our modern canary carcasses and ourselves. Some of us even think the canaries are the problem. The danger signals blaring all around us don't seem to mean anything. We have become deaf to the portents of danger, treating them like the car alarms that we routinely ignore on our urban streets.

If we are to stop our headlong rush to destruction, we must change the way we think and the way we act. It is time to attend to the canaries.

Our social and ecological statistics are telling us what we already know in our hearts: we have created a world that works for only a few. It does not even work for those it purports to serve. To change this, we must learn to act toward each other and our environment in profoundly different ways.

Though our crises have their roots in the distant past, we who are now living are all, paradoxically, responsible for them. Every day, you contribute to the mess. So do I. Collectively, we reinvent this society daily. Some of us may have more historical responsibility for our present conditions than others, but at this point it does not matter who set the house on fire, who carried the gasoline, and whether the blaze was accidental, intentional, or the result of gross negligence or stupidity. What matters most is that we figure out how to quench the flames.

The Central Theme

Our present world works for only a few. However, by shifting our consciousness, then our culture and institutions, we can create a world that works for all.

This theme will be developed as we move through the three parts of this book:

Envisioning an Inclusive World

From our earliest years, we are taught that the world is limited and cannot work for all. This is a prime assumption of our present society. Part One turns that assumption on its ear. Before providing an overview of what I call *The Mess*—our interlocked and mutually reinforcing problems, challenges, and crises—the book introduces the concept of *inclusivity*, the notion that our lives are inextricably linked to each other. Inclusivity is the basis for a world that works for all.

A New Analysis for a New Society

The accuracy of our vision depends on our tools of analysis. Most of us use analyses that are centuries old and based on flawed concepts of how the world works. For example, our present expenditure of billions of dollars on the Human Genome Project is based on the limiting Cartesian belief that the human body is a machine that can be understood best by taking it apart.

Part Two analyzes our analysis. It examines our need for a new *story* that will help us heal our society. A story is not a nursery tale, myth, or fable but the operative blueprint of how we function as a society. It reveals the rationale for our acting the way we do. Changing our story is the fastest and most effective way to change our world.

Part Two explores in depth the three major stories that have shaped the behavior of humans on this planet:

The Original Story: "The Keepers"

The Dominant Story: "The Breakers"

The Emerging Story: "The Menders"

The Breaker story, which tries hard to be the *only* story, has the subtitle "Creating a World that Works for Me." This story is based on a thought, "I am separate," and an assumption, "There is not enough." Breakers are people who live disconnected from the Earth, from local ecologies, and from all other beings. Their consciousness breaks relationships at every level of existence.

Operating from within the Breaker story, humans try to control all aspects of life on Earth. This control is, among other things, military, political, economic, ecological, genetic, and scientific. It is the root of every one of our pervasive and interlocking global crises. Breaker thought, in other words, creates The Mess.

Breakers, although great at manipulating the physical environment, are largely blind to spiritual realities. Their "I am separate" consciousness lies behind the demoralization, disenchantment, and spiritual starvation of our society.

Things have not always been like this. For over one million years, humans had another way: "Living in harmony with all I encounter." This is the story of the Keepers, the indigenous people of the Earth. Keepers were, and still are, in intimate connection with their local ecologies and all other beings. They have maintained the ancient ways of living, perfected over millennia of coexistence.

Part Two introduces us, finally, to the emerging Menders story: "Creating a World That Works for All." Menders are people who choose to live as conscious, integral parts of a vital, sacred planet. Their fundamental thought is "We are One," and their guiding assumption is "There is enough for all." Menders are functioning as the catalysts of a new society, consciously creating alternatives to Breaker excesses. Menders recognize that we can begin the process of restoring balance to the Earth and to ourselves *in this generation*. This book is for those catalysts.

Being a Mender is a spiritual discipline. As Menders, our focus is on a world greater than our individual personalities, families, or nations, greater than our sensory world. We act not just for ourselves, not just for other beings currently cohabiting the Earth with us, but also for future generations and for the Earth herself.

The Revolution to Inclusivity

Right now, the most widespread tools of social change on our planet include bullets and bombs. Regardless of the delivery system (a B-52 bomber dropping cruise missiles or a suicide bomber on a crowded bus), the primary method of changing consciousness is to silence those who disagree. But at the onset of the new millennium, we are beginning to realize that fear, slaughter, and oppression are ineffective as tools of social change. We are beginning to understand the operation of inclusivity: anything I do to

The Other comes back to affect my life. Seeing our lives as inextricably linked will bring us to nonviolence.

Understanding the problem is not enough. Even articulating a new story is not enough. If we are going to create a world that works for all, we have to take practical steps to manifest our story. Part Three explores these steps to the Mender era.

The Bell That Tolls for Thee

You may be wondering whether I am being alarmist. Or you may feel certain that I am exaggerating our problems. Things can't be that bad. Many of the Earth's ills have already been eliminated, and we'll take care of the rest soon. Perhaps you think that because I have had a hard life, I am inflating the difficulties faced by the rest of the world. Your own life is going pretty well. You have steady work you enjoy, comfortable living quarters, a loving family. You may think I need to "get over it." Well, if you choose to believe that if something has not affected you, it *cannot* affect you, this probably is not your book.

However serene your life may be, it can be shattered by any of a number of events triggered by The Mess:

- Suicide, or attempted suicide, by a loved one
- An attack by muggers that leaves you or someone close to you seriously injured
- Your child sickened by an industrial pollutant in the soil, air, or water
- A member of your family killed or maimed in a terrorist attack
- The discovery that someone you love is addicted to drugs

You will then start asking yourself some questions. What did I do wrong? How could I have been so blind? What is this world coming to? Why did this have to happen? What does it mean? In the context of such questions, this book will begin to make sense.

There are many books on the market that are designed to make you feel good, that are written to entertain you, to help you feel smug in your superiority over the "bad guys." This is not intended to be one of them. Although, by the end of the book, I sincerely hope you will share my sense of optimism and excitement about our future, along the way you will be asked to explore some of the suppressed and unpleasant aspects of yourself and your actions.

This is your book if you understand that the conditions that affect any of us affect all of us. Regardless of whether I personally have been robbed or raped, I can still desire to create a society where robbery, rape, and all of our other social maladies are unthinkable.

Terminology and Names

A glossary of specialized terms is provided at the end of the book, but one term needs a brief comment here. When I speak of *America,* I am referring neither to all the countries of the continent nor to the United States as a political and geographic entity. I use the word to refer to a *culture* and *consciousness* that most people in the world have no trouble identifying as "American." Under this definition, Americans are those people, regardless of whether they are citizens of the United States, who demonstrate certain identifiable cultural beliefs and values.

America is the driving force behind the worldwide spread of Breaker consciousness in our era. Americans are the trouble that is troubling the world. Therefore, this book focuses primarily on what Americans are now doing and what we can do differently.

Another point: the text sometimes speaks of "you," sometimes of "I," and often of "we." Focusing solely on "you" might have given the false impression that I did not share the experiences I was discussing. Speaking exclusively in the first person would have created the impression that the book was an autobiographical cathartic confession and that I was *not* talking about you. And if every statement had been couched in terms of "we," you might have wondered exactly whom I was talking to and about. My solution has been to mix all three vantage points. However, when reading the text, feel free to change the pronouns and see how that affects your understanding of what is being said.

Finally, most of the people I mention in this book—friends, workshop participants, and others—appear under fictitious names (and sometimes genders) so that they can retain their privacy. The only exceptions are individuals who gave permission for their true names to be used or whose actions are a matter of public knowledge.

PART ONE

Envisioning an Inclusive World

A human being is part of the whole, called by us "universe," a part limited in time and space. He experiences himself, his thoughts and feelings, as something separated from the rest—a kind of delusion of his consciousness. This delusion is a prison for us, restricting us to our personal desires and to affection for a few persons nearest to us. Our task must be to free ourselves from this prison by widening our circle of compassion to embrace all living creatures and the whole of nature in its beauty.

—ALBERT EINSTEIN[3]

1

THE VISION

[O]ur greatest strength lies not in how much we differ from each other but in how much—how very much—we are the same.
—EKNATH EASWARAN[4]

WHEN YOU WOKE UP this morning, you had a series of goals. Some were as simple as turning off the alarm clock, brushing your teeth, making sure you got to work on time. Other goals may have been more ambitious—writing the résumé that would land the perfect job, buying the right food for an important dinner, sitting in meditation for the sake of enlightenment. Your goals include the ordinary, the sublime, and everything in between.

Like people, societies also have goals. Some are as simple as making sure everyone has decent water to drink; others may be as complex as landing an astronaut on Mars.

Our goal used to be simple—stop Soviet expansion. The implosion of the Soviet Union also imploded our goal. Now, at the turn of the millennium, we must ask ourselves: What are we trying to achieve as a society? Without defining what we are against, what are we for? Goal setting is important: without a clear vision of an achievable goal, and an understanding of the philosophy and values behind that goal, we run the risk of becoming sidetracked, confused, burned out, or cynical.

The Essence of Inclusivity

Simply put, the Mender goal is *an inclusive human society on a habitable planet,* a society that works for all humans and for all nonhumans. This means fulfillment both for those who are at the top of the society and for those at the bottom. Work, resources, responsibilities, spiritual gifts, and material goods may not be evenly spread, but everyone has "enough"; anyone could trade places with anyone else without feeling deprived or oppressed. Such a society is essentially benign and healing to both the human and the more-than-human world.[5]

All beings, all things, are One. Our lives are inextricably linked one to another. Because of this, we cannot wage war against anything or anyone without waging war against ourselves. Therefore, we are obliged to treat all beings the way we want to be treated. There are no "enemies"—all beings are expressions of the Sacred and must be treated as such. Some beings cause pain to others; this does not mean that they are enemies. Some beings are food for others; this is all the more reason to treat them as sacred. Once we understand that we are interconnected, we have the responsibility to create a world that works for all.

With this as our goal, the next question is obvious: how do we achieve it? How do we avoid sinking into despair or cynicism? And how do we avoid dabbling in utopian fantasies or engaging in "pie-in-the-sky" religiosity? In fact, we can change this world right now by shifting our consciousness and our values from a foundation of exclusivity to one of inclusivity.

This shift in consciousness is the core of the world's major religions. The essence of the moral code they urge upon us is inclusivity.

What is hateful to you, do not do to others.

—RABBI HILLEL

Do not hurt others with that which hurts yourself.

—BUDDHA

Do unto others whatever you would have them do unto you.

—JESUS

None of you is a believer until you love for your neighbor what you love for yourself.

—MUHAMMAD

Considering the clarity, simplicity, and consistency of these statements, one has to wonder what it is about the message of inclusivity that makes it nearly impossible for people to either comprehend or implement. Why are there Jews, Buddhists, Christians, Muslims, and many others around the world who are killing their fellow men and women when their traditions call for peace, nonviolence, and inclusivity? We will face these questions as we explore inclusivity in the following chapters.

A Turning Point

Do you feel the promise in these perilous times? Despite our many challenges, do these times feel hopeful to you in some way? Does it seem to you that something is ready to change? How are we going to capture the promise that lies within our present predicament as we stand on the brink of the twenty-first century?

The hard fact is that getting to a world that works for all will take a more rigorous analysis and more sophisticated actions, both internal and external, than our current political, social, and even spiritual leaders are advocating. It will take fundamental change that must originate with you, as an emerging leader of the new millennium. If our current leadership were capable of it, they would have done it by now.

Such change does not take place at the surface, but deep within. It is already at work. We are all a part of it. The ice breaking on a frozen river is an indication of warming trends and currents that have been at work for a long time. The breakup at the surface is the culmination of a process, not its beginning. The breakup of ice on a river, the emergence of a butterfly from its chrysalis, a Declaration of Independence, each culminates a process that has preceded it by days or decades.

Prerequisites of Change

One of the mistakes many of us made in the Sixties was thinking we all just had to love each other and the evil system would go away. Despite our good intentions and hard work, we did not understand the processes of societal change. And we were at the mercy of those who did understand.

Systemic change does not miraculously bubble up from a change of heart. It is intentional, stemming from a precise and rigorous examination of present conditions and an understanding of the consciousness and spirit from which those conditions have emerged.

When Karl Marx analyzed capitalism, he did so with the same consciousness that created capitalism in the first place. Marx, as a Breaker scientist, saw an "I am separate" world, a world of limited resources, a world in dire need of human domination and control. This is what his consciousness was trained to see, and the system of communism was built upon that consciousness. He and Friedrich Engels inspired the creation of a political structure controlled by a small elite, an industrial empire that ecologically devastated the land, sea, and air in its never-ending quest for more resources. The system created by Marx's disciples Lenin and Stalin killed, jailed, tortured, and oppressed millions while being blind to its own contradictions or the aspirations of its people.

Communism was merely another manifestation of Breaker consciousness. What looked like a different system was only a different way of looking at the same system. Marx analyzed the conditions but not the consciousness. Same wine in a slightly different bottle.

What Is Exclusivity?

Exclusivity is the notion that "I" am separate from "you" (or any "Other"). This notion is what Einstein called a delusion of consciousness, a delusion that imprisons us. No beings other than humans suffer this delusion. And not all humans see themselves as separated entities. As we shall explore further, indigenous people see themselves as an integral part of their local ecology, making the notion of selling land as absurd to them as selling parts of their bodies.

In itself, exclusivity is not bad; the problem is being imprisoned in this myopic way of viewing self and world. A surgeon operates on her patient from an "I am separate" perspective, having the objectivity to cut open and manipulate the patient's body. From the patient's point of view, objectivity is a good thing.

Exclusivity is the root of all of our human maladies. It allows us not only to separate from others but also to oppress them. Racism, sexism, homophobia, slavery, all forms of hatred and bigotry, stem from the notion "I am separate from you—by virtue of skin color, ethnicity, behavior, belief . . ." It is exclusivity that allows a bomber to kill unarmed civilians—whether a suicide bomber on a bus in Sri Lanka or an Air Force bomber dropping an atomic weapon on a city. Of the 110 million deaths from wars in this century, two-thirds of them, 73 million, have been of civilians.[6] For the proponents of exclusivity, this has been a very active century.

According to the teachings of exclusivity, a society that works for all is impossible. The Breaker story holds that a restructuring of our priorities and our consciousness is impossible. The status quo is called "human nature." Everything we have learned in formal education and in our culture reinforces the notion that the world can work for only a few. History, anthropology, psychology, politics, economics—and our fathers and mothers—strengthen the idea that the world cannot work for all.

Think back to your first economics course. On the first day, the teacher or professor said something like, "Economics is the allocation of limited resources." You didn't question it, you dutifully wrote it down—it fit your world picture. That laid the groundwork for all the later explanations of why some were millionaires while others were permanently unemployed.

Both winners and losers tend to believe that the world is limited and can work only for a few. Those on the bottom seek to make someone else lose rather than questioning the assumptions built into the system.

As Menders, we believe that an inclusive society is not only possible but is achievable *right now,* with the resources presently available to us. We don't have to wait for more resources or better technology. For example, we know that every year, America produces enough grain to feed every hungry person in the world, and has the means to distribute it. We do not need more technological advances to feed starving people; we need a change of heart that leads to changes in our priorities and systems.

A world that works for all is *not* achievable without restructuring our priorities, our attitudes, and our culture. We cannot tinker with this; the change must be fundamental—an evolutionary shift toward spiritual compassion, and corresponding shifts in our actions. In short, a transformation of head, heart, and hand.

We must work on ourselves first, and then be prepared to do the work on our culture and institutions. As we will see in Chapter 3, the essence of this work is spiritual, part of our quest for the reality that transcends our ordinary experience.

The Three Criteria of a World That Works for All

How can we tell when we have reached our goal? How do we know when we've "won"?

In the realm of personal goals, the point of achievement is usually clear: you sign your name to a finished canvas, count your winnings from a slot machine. Some of our societal goals are also easy to measure. For example, America's goal was to put a man on the Moon. Ten years later, Neil Armstrong walked on the Moon. Goal achieved. However, other societal goals are impossible to measure. If we choose a goal like "absolute equality," we are setting ourselves up for disappointment, despair, burnout, and the illnesses associated with long-term frustration. A more reasonable goal than absolute equality is "full voting and civil rights for all Americans."

Conversely, setting goals too narrowly leads us to slip into a "quick win" syndrome and can be a precursor to cynicism, shallowness, and hollow achievements. "Defeat House Bill 2931-6B" does nothing to rouse our spirits to action.

Is "a world that works for all" an unmeasurable goal? What would such a world look like? The proverbial "a chicken in every pot and a car in every garage"? Universal color television for the world? Everybody with a job? Internet access for all? Clean water and decent food? In fact, none of these achievements would, in itself, indicate that we were living in a world that works for all.

For years, I knew intuitively that the world could work for all but did not know the criteria for such a state of affairs. Nor did I have any concrete examples of how such a world would operate, especially in a multicultural setting. I was particularly troubled that neither the implied meritocracy of capitalism nor the professed egalitarian ideals of communism were sufficient, on their own, to create a world that works for all. In order to discover the criteria for inclusivity, it was necessary to move beyond the confines of exclusive thinking.

Then, in 1997, on the other side of the planet, I witnessed a practical demonstration of a world that works for all.

The Sarvodaya Canteen

Twice in 1997 I visited the beautiful but war-torn island of Sri Lanka, to work with and learn from Dr. A. T. Ariyaratne, founder and president of the Sarvodaya Shramadana Movement. Sarvodaya began humbly forty years ago, when "Ari," as a young high school teacher, took some of his students to poor villages to donate their labor. Since that time, Sarvodaya has become a large self-help development movement based on Buddhist and Gandhian principles, whose undertakings include orphanages for battered children, rural water and solar energy projects, legal services, women's projects, economic development, Grameen-style micro-lending banks, and more. I learned much from the little man with the warm smile who is widely regarded as "the living Gandhi."

It was in the Sarvodaya canteen that I could see a microcosm of a world that worked for all. For Sarvodaya workers and the foreign volunteers that the organization attracts from around the world, the canteen is a meeting place. They gather there for their meals and, twice a day, for supersweet British-style tea. Lunch is the grand confluence, with hundreds of workers, volunteers, and visitors sharing a meal.

In the canteen, foreigners are treated differently from the native Sri Lankans. To summarize the differences:

- Foreigners (visitors and workers) eat from china plates; Sri Lankans eat from wide, shallow bowls made of metal.
- Foreigners get served at a special table reserved for them; Sri Lankans eat at all the other tables.
- Foreigners are served "family style" from platters of food. Generally, they have twice as much food available as any human being could possibly eat. (If eating alone, a person

is served enough food for two on the platters; a group of six is served enough for twelve.) Sri Lankans get their food by going to the kitchen door, where they are given a plate heaped with rice and all of the same curries that are found on the foreigners' table. If they are still hungry after eating their first serving, they simply go back to the kitchen door for another plate of food.

After observing this system carefully, I came to the conclusion that it provided the best way to serve a large group of people representing different cultures, different gastronomic capacities and tastes, and different eating styles and habits.

Some Westerners, especially Americans who have been through "diversity training," see things differently. They loudly protest the "privileges" of having "more food," china plates, and table service. A few, totally disregarding Sri Lankan culture and courtesy, will try to get their food in the kitchen line, which confuses everybody. (Because it is a Sri Lankan custom to offer abundant food and hospitality to guests, the Americans who try to be "culturally correct" will *still* find a china plate and generous servings waiting for them after they have stood in line for a Sri Lankan plate!)

I remind the Western guests who want to reject their perceived "privileges" in food distribution that the system *works for the Sri Lankans.* It works because of three principal factors:

Criterion 1: Enoughness. Everyone has enough, even though resources are not shared equally. No one in the Sarvodaya canteen walks out hungry. Any Sri Lankan who wants more can easily get more. But in fact the initial portions are very generous and few people go back for seconds. Ask any Sri Lankan Sarvodaya worker, "Do you have enough food?" The answer is invariably "Oh, yes!"

Criterion 2: Exchangeability. Trading places would be okay. If foreigners and Sri Lankans swapped places in the canteen, no one would feel deprived. The Sri Lankans, "forced" to eat from china plates, would be okay about it. The Westerners, "compelled" to line up at the kitchen door for their food, would make no complaint. (Exchangeability does not mean everyone would *like* or *prefer* the change. It means people would not feel they were being punished or stigmatized—or unjustly rewarded—by the change.)

Criterion 3: Common Benefit. The system is designed and intended to benefit all. No one is harmed by the Sarvodaya system; everyone benefits, even though some of the Westerners may not grasp this.

The Sri Lankans came up with the system for good, practical reasons, not because they are subservient or need to suck up to Westerners. Putting food on someone's plate that they cannot or will not eat is a waste; putting it on platters lets the Westerners take as much or as little as they want. Offering guests abundant food is a cultural trait. Sri Lankans do this with each other in the villages. Why change the courtesy just because the guest is from another country?

If everyone has enough, if trading places would be okay, and if the system has been designed to benefit everyone, we have created something powerful: a world that works for all!

Applying the Criteria

Apply the three criteria to *any* of our current domestic or foreign issues and see how you judge them:

- Does the world work for a welfare mother? Does she have enough? Would you trade places with her? Was the welfare system designed to benefit her? (If you are inclined to answer yes to the last question, think again. No person in need of assistance would ever have designed a system that institutionalized poverty and despair for generations.)

- Does the world work for all the residents of your city? Would you be willing to trade places with someone on the other side of town? Would it be "safe" for you to do so? Do the residents of your city have enough security? Were your city's institutions designed to benefit every citizen?

- Does the world work for a teenager who just attempted suicide? Does he have enough—in this case, enough love, understanding, respect or self-esteem? Would you trade places with him? Were local social and psychiatric services designed to benefit all age groups?

- Does the world work for a tree in an old growth forest, about to be cut down to feed the insatiable appetites of Breakers for more *things?* Does it have enough . . . life? Would you trade places and offer yourself for sacrifice to satisfy someone's greed? Was the system designed to benefit this tree, or any tree?

- Does the world work for the average Iraqi citizen, oppressed on the ground by a ruthless regime and oppressed from above by U.S. warplanes dropping "smart" bombs? Does she have enough security? Is any part of her political life designed to benefit her? Would you trade places with her?

- Does this world work for our children? Do they have enough future? Would you trade places with them, given the risks, dangers, and uncertainties of the twenty-first century? Was the system through which we squandered their inheritance of resources while saddling them with our debts designed to benefit them?

We can apply the three criteria as we consider whether our current institutions or our proposed solutions are actually capable of reaching our goals.

A Paradoxical Moment

We find ourselves at a confusing crossroads: we know the old Breaker society does not work, but we have not yet created a new Mender society with which to replace it. As a result, paradoxes abound. Almost every major college in the United States now has a department or school of ecology, environmental studies, or earth sciences, yet major timber companies are still legally clearcutting forests at the rate of 16 million hectares per year.[7] While the U.S. government spends money to discourage people from smoking and to treat those suffering from tobacco-related diseases, it also devotes millions of public dollars to the artificial support of tobacco prices.

At a transitional point such as this, it is all too easy to lose your sense of direction or lose heart. The imperative is to keep your fundamental intention clearly in mind and to doggedly pursue it. Over time, the old will yield to the new.

Our Problems Are Blessings

The unleashed power of the atom has changed everything except our modes of thinking, and thus we drift toward unparalleled catastrophes. We shall require a substantially new manner of thinking if humanity is to survive.

—ALBERT EINSTEIN[8]

Our problems are blessings in disguise, because they are leading us to think about solving our problems in very different ways. The complexity of The Mess is the impetus to search for more fundamental solutions.

Tumbleweed Dream

Recently I had a "teaching dream." Most of my dreams are personal, but others are meant to be shared with those who appear in them, and still others are clearly intended as teaching tools. This is one of the teaching dreams.

THE DREAM

In this dream, I am both Observer and Participant. I am on a road, blindfolded. As the Observer, I can see myself from above, standing on the road. As the Participant, I feel myself blindfolded and helpless. I am in a place like Kansas, with broad horizons and wide open spaces. Behind me there's a huge tumbleweed, rolling down the road. The scraping sound of this tumbleweed coming my way scares me, so I start running, still blindfolded. As I run faster, the tumbleweed picks up speed. I (the Participant) don't know what it is, or whether it can hurt me.

I run off a high cliff, the tumbleweed still in pursuit. I am in the air, falling. I am still trying to avoid the tumbleweed; I am afraid of being smashed on the ground. I am still blindfolded, so I don't know how far away the ground is.

As I am falling, I hear voices calling out to me: "Take off your blindfold and fly along with us!" I am afraid to take off the blindfold. I don't trust the voices. I don't believe people can fly. I know I am going to die; the blindfold protects me from the certainty of the moment of my death. Even though I know I will die, I still want to pretend that my death will be a surprise.

Although I am afraid, I remove the blindfold. I see people, thousands upon thousands of people, dressed in strange clothes, slowly flying around me. I am the only one falling. They say to me: "Follow our ways and you too will fly!" Their ways are foreign to me, but I do not see the alternative. As I follow them, the road, the blindfold, the tumbleweed are left behind, forgotten. The fear of crashing is a vague memory. I am flying.

This dream is worth pondering. What would have happened if I had taken off the blindfold on the road? Before the cliff? I would have avoided the tumbleweed and the cliff edge, but never learned that I could fly. Paradoxically, if I had resolved my problems too soon, I would never have experienced transformation. My problems really were a blessing.

I see the Tumbleweed Dream as a powerful metaphor for the state of our society. We are blessed with our problems—blessed with poverty, with social decay, with The Mess. These conditions impel us to new, inclusive ways to connect ourselves with others. We are, in our "blind" state, being impelled to change, to grow.

What was the tumbleweed in the dream? The tumbleweed represented *fear*. This powerful image of impending doom was necessary to get me to jump off the cliff. Our fear leads us to take actions of which we have previously believed ourselves incapable.

The blindfold represented ignorance. Who put that blindfold on me? Perhaps it was self-imposed; or perhaps someone did it for my own good. Perhaps the blindfold is a form of divine intervention, a process (like childbirth) outside of my conscious control that is for the good of life. Whatever it was, it got me to fly.

Baby Bird in the Nest

Our interlocking personal, environmental, and social crises are like a mother bird pushing her young out of the nest when it is ready to fly.

Is this forcible ejection from the nest an act of cruelty or an act of love? It depends on which bird you talk to. From the point of view of the chick clinging to the side of the nest, or on her way down to the ground, being pushed is cruel. The baby bird detests this disruption of her cozy life.

However, we know that the mother bird is acting out of the depths of her love for the chick. She knows the capacity of her offspring, knows when it is time for the chick to fully mature. She cannot talk the chick into flying: "Cindy, those things hanging at your sides are wings, like mine. Just flap them and you'll fly like me!" Yeah, sure.

The mother bird built her nest far enough from the ground that the baby would have plenty of time to figure out flying before impact. Building the nest up high, along with pushing the chick out, are acts of love. The baby bird has to be high enough to do three things:

- Recognize that she is facing imminent death.
- Quickly learn some basic principles of aerodynamics.
- Apply the principles before she hits the ground.

Our problems, like those of the falling chick, are so overwhelming that we are forced to find a new way of acting, to spread wings that we did not know we had. We've got a little way to go before impact—just enough time to figure out what we must do to avert a terminal splat.

Remembering that our problems provide the impetus for fundamental change allows us to remain optimistic about our future, despite The Mess. Things can and will get better, for us all.

2

The Nightmare—
A World on the Brink

I can remember staring at the golden goblet, the one with the huge jewels encrusting its fluted base. Holding it in my hand as first acolyte during Sunday services at St. John's Episcopal Church, I was surprised at how heavy it was. From matching gold pitchers I would pour the wine and water for the Sacrament.

I can remember my first reaction to handling the hardware of Communion. I felt neither awe nor envy—just a cool calculation of exactly how many poor people could be housed and fed with the money that the church had invested in a glorified wineglass.

Every day, I got to wake up to the bedroom I shared with my older brother, the room with the partially collapsed wall, the one that took in water when it rained. We put up plastic sheets to keep the moisture and the smells from aggravating my already severe asthma.

Four of us lived in a two-bedroom row house a few blocks from the church. My younger sister slept with our mother. (Although this may sound crowded to you, we had just moved from a studio apartment, all of us sharing one room.) Once a week, for less than an hour, I got to be near a cup that would have paid for a fully rehabilitated house for us—and about twenty of our neighbors.

I can remember asking the Sunday School teacher, "Wouldn't Jesus want us to do Communion with paper cups, and use the money to feed people or give them a good place to live?"

I also remember his reply: "You're too young to understand these things." (And, I am happy to say, after almost forty years, I am still too young to understand.)

At ten years old, all I knew was that the world didn't work.

THE WORLD IS A MESS. We are in deep trouble. We can see this everywhere we look. Africa is racked by AIDS and neverending low-level warfare. Russia is in economic and political turmoil. Asia is attempting to piece together its financial institutions following the catastrophe of 1998. America is coming apart at the seams, torn by race, class, ideology and more. Our times cry out for change. We live in a world that works for only a few.

This wasn't always true. And it doesn't have to be true now.

Most of you already know this. The fact that you are reading this book probably means you are looking for solutions, not wondering whether a problem exists. You may not know the full magnitude of our problems. In fact, you cannot. No one can fully comprehend "The Mess." But you do know that the present world does not work, and doesn't work in some profound ways. It's not like a car that needs a tune-up; it's like a car that has failed brakes and is heading downhill, picking up speed, with a truck full of gasoline on the right, a school bus packed with children on the left, and a cliff straight ahead. The times compel us to act, but do not give us many options. If we are not acting on the problems, it is not because we don't see them but because we don't know what to do about them.

I do not know what path led you to this point in your life. You may have arrived by the politics of the Left or the Right. You may have gotten here through traditional religion or by rejecting such traditions. You may have realized that we are not going to consume our way out of our problems. You may have discovered that neither conventional political activism nor apathy has created a world that works. You may have become cynical, or even considered radically dropping out through suicide, drugs, or other forms of self-violence. The path that brought you here does not matter. What matters is that you have come to see that something profound needs to change.

The Problem Without a Name

Our societal and personal problems are so fundamental, nightmarish, complex, and interlocked that they are incapable of being addressed with our current techniques of problem solving. These challenges are so difficult to grasp in part because we do not have a word that defines them.

In his classic book, *The Timeless Way of Building,*[9] master architect Christopher Alexander refers to a quality in our lives that is the source of our aliveness, our beauty, our creativity and joy of living. He called this "the quality without a name," since it was impossible to render it into words. But although we cannot name it, we can know it.

There is an equal and opposite quality to the one Alexander identified: it is the quality of our pain, our ugliness, our cynicism, brutality, coldheartedness, and violence. Alexander would probably call it "the problem without a name." I call it "The Mess."

Every year, scores of respected research institutes give us their latest updates on how much closer to crisis our world has come. From the Worldwatch Institute, the Hunger Project, Amnesty International, World Resources Institute, Oxfam, Doctors Without

Borders, UNICEF, Human Rights Watch, and literally dozens more like them, we get a composite picture of the depth and magnitude of The Mess. They each report on one aspect of it. You are no doubt already aware of their work; if not, please refer to their clear and unambiguous reporting of our troubles and trends.

The Mess includes

Population explosion
Suicide
Holes in the ozone layer
Political corruption
Homelessness
Emotional stress
Destruction of cultures
Overgrazing
Use of children as combatants
 in warfare
Violent political conflict
Spiritual emptiness
Acid rain
Pandemics
Decline in basic values
Teenage pregnancy
Increasing disparities in wealth
Racism
Wage slavery
Chemical, biological, nuclear, and
 other weapons of mass destruction
AIDS
Ethnic unrest and conflict
Civil wars
Public school violence
Spreading desertification
Political and social alienation

Extinction of species
Sexism
Overuse of fertilizers/pesticides
Global climate change
Expanding global corporatism
Destruction of family life
Colonialism and neocolonialism
Homicide
Political apathy and malaise
Attention deficit and other
 mental disorders in children
Terrorism
Unsustainability in all aspects
 of life
Militarization of outer space
Genocide
Cancer, especially in children
Economic and class disparities
War between nations
Overconsumption
Urban deterioration
Regional famines
Destruction of the natural
 environment
Crime
Child slave labor
Industrial pollution

These problems, and numerous others not listed, are not separate elements, but symptoms of a single condition, parts of The Mess. The items are listed at random and without categorization. This is purposeful. The mind tries to find order and patterns. The lack of traditional categories is an invitation to shift our consciousness into new, expanded frameworks. In this case, you are invited to think outside the usual categories such as "ecological," "political," and "cultural." The problems that constitute The Mess connect to each other in startling and unpredictable ways. Categories would blind you to many of these connections. How many people, for example, are aware of the causal link between Iraq's "political" act of setting fire to the Kuwaiti oil fields during the Gulf War and exacerbated air and water ("ecological") problems throughout the Middle East?

Open your eyes to these connections. Go back and read the list out loud. See if you have a different reaction to the enormity of our global predicament. Or look at any two conditions and ask yourself: "In what ways does the first relate to the second?" Allow your heart, your imagination to discover the connections that were not obvious from your initial reading.

All parts of The Mess are interconnected. Focusing on one part alone means the others are allowed to fester. Curing racism or child abuse or environmental degradation alone would only mean that Breaker "I am separate" thinking would grow stronger somewhere else. The world still wouldn't work for all. It's time that we tackled the *problem,* not the *pieces.*

Right now, Breakers are pointing fingers at each other, trying to assign blame for sexism, for declining fish populations, for racism, for child abuse, for The Mess as a whole. (For example, Democrats and Republicans each blame the other for urban violence, citing either failed social policies or a lack of gun control.) But the culprits aren't male chauvinists, overfishing, poor child rearing, welfare, Republicans, Democrats, or any of the other specific manifestations of exclusivity. The problem is the Breaker story itself, the consciousness that *gives* us sexism, overfishing, poor child rearing, welfare, and so on.

The world does not have to be a mess. We can, right now, with our presently available resources, create a world that works for all. As I said in *The Power of One: Authentic Leadership in Turbulent Times*,[10] one person, acting out of the power of his or her deepest convictions, can change the world. The power to transform our world, the power of revolution, lies with you. So does the responsibility. Refusing to recognize your power, giving your power to others, or focusing all of your attention on another's power means that you will be ineffective in the world.

However, the Power of One does not mean that anything you choose to do will be effective. First of all, you must know what's wrong. Although I know automotive theory, I'm not capable of diagnosing every malfunction of my car. If my car engine is that complicated, how can we change this engine called America, with its 260 million moving parts?

Not knowing what to do, we deny, ignore, or request "further studies" of the problems. Meanwhile, The Mess gets messier.

THE ANT COLONY

Among the many exhibits in Washington's Smithsonian Institution is an active colony of leaf-cutter ants, housed at the National Zoo.

From time to time, the ant queen has to change her location, and the ants that serve her may help transport her from one place to another.

One day, according to Ed Smith of the National Zoo staff, the helper ants were assisting the queen in her transit to another chamber. The problem was that her present chamber had been purposely designed by her human keepers to prevent any such exit. But the helper ants were persistent. They would not give up on their efforts to get her through an opening that was too small for her body. And in pulling and pulling, they yanked off her head.

What effect do you think the decapitation of the queen had on the ant community?

For weeks, they didn't notice the difference.

The ants whose task it was to take eggs from the queen to the hatching chamber now went to her dead body, didn't get an egg, returned to the hatching chamber, then went back for another nonexistent egg. The ants that had the job of feeding the queen carried food to the decapitated head. The food went uneaten, so they carried it back out and brought more food in.

But over time they moved more and more slowly, finally stopping in place. According to another zoo staffperson: "The daughters all stood around, waiting for something to happen. It looked like the Great Depression in America."

Because ants are cold-blooded, with a very low metabolism, they did not starve. They lived out their lives, still standing and waiting.

Just like the ants, most of us are going through the accustomed motions. At some point, we lost the central focus of our society. Once, it was rebellion against a king; later, geographic expansion; then industrial expansion, followed by the struggle against Nazism and, most recently, the long, hostile standoff with Soviet communism. Now that the "Evil Empire" has collapsed, what overriding goal do we have as a nation? Are we not drifting without a purpose? We have "pulled the head off" and are now mechanically serving the dead body politic. We *know* it does not work, but still act as though it did.

I can't remember at what point I first realized that the world didn't work for me . . . certainly I was in the single digits. Things stood out as being wrong. I lacked the ability to analyze my conditions or articulate a reason, but my heart needed no words to distinguish right from wrong.

I was around nine years old, standing on the front steps of a house my mother was about to rent, staring up at a red sticker posted on the front door. It had the official seal of the City of Camden. I had just gotten past the word "DANGER" and was trying to read the rest of the message when the landlord, a fat man who seemed to be my height, saw me looking at the red sticker. He walked over and tore it down. "Don't worry about it, kid," he said, turning back to my mother, who at six feet towered over both of us. I knew she saw the sign. I also knew, as my siblings knew, that she was doing the best she could.

This condemned house on Benson Street was where my five-year-old sister went over the side of the rickety fire escape from the second floor, landing on her face and splitting her tongue in two on the broken wine and beer bottles that littered the alleyway, our playground. Tearing that sticker off did not make the house safe, it just made it available.

America is the world's single biggest problem. But paradoxically, America is also the world's single greatest hope. If we can make an inclusive society work here, we will then be poised to share our new story with the world. Some of us are trying to find a new "head," a new paradigm, a new way of looking at our society. Later in this book, we will begin to compose a new story, the Mender story, which tells of a world that works for all.

Nightmares of the Present

I am not a futurist. One doesn't have to be able to foretell the future to know that we have deep problems right now.

Most of the time, we do not see the totality of our problem. As an ant in my garden cannot see the garden, none of us can truly see The Mess. We focus on our little corner to the exclusion of others. And if our corner is okay, we act as if The Mess did not exist at all.

If we are going to create a world that works for all, we have to first see how the world does not work. The following nightmare scenarios are offered not to lock you into despair but simply to demonstrate that our solutions must be as deep as our problems and challenges. These scenarios show how omnipresent our problems are, and how fundamental our solutions must be. As you read this section, please remember: these nightmares are all parts of the same problem, different aspects of The Mess.

A Child of The Mess

The world is turning out billions of people who are scarred in some way by The Mess. I am one of them.

I have the dubious honor of having been raised in Camden, New Jersey. A few years ago, *Time* magazine made official what anyone who had ever visited Camden already knew: Camden is the worst city in America. We beat out places like East St. Louis and Gary, Indiana. (There are no bragging rights associated with being from the second worst city in America.)

Camden is far worse than any of the reporters who dive in for a quick story can ever realize. And far worse than I'm going to talk about now. Just thank God you (probably) don't have a frame of reference to comprehend the reality of Camden.

> When I attended Pyne Poynt Junior High School, several of us had a unique "game" that we called "Coat Jobs." We would get our coats early from our lockers, then stand along the wall on the long main corridor. Suddenly and at random, one of us would throw his coat over the head of one of the passersby and the rest of us would beat the unsuspecting student into the ground.

Usually, we would not know, or care, who was under the coat. Though we steered away from girls, everyone else was fair game. It did not matter to us whether the person under the coat was white, black, or Hispanic. It did not matter if he was older or younger. The violence gave us a temporary release from our emptiness.

One of the terrible truths of growing up in Camden is that, from the inside, the horrors look normal. In my book, *The Power of One,* there is a story about Frog Soup: drop a frog into lukewarm water, slowly raise the temperature, and the frog will just sit there and boil to death. Camden is a city of frogs, all oblivious to the rising temperature.

I learned how to square dance in the sixth grade in the concrete exercise yard at Broadway School, crunching broken glass and plastic heroin envelopes underfoot in a do-si-do that we assumed was the norm. The fact that we never saw Wally or The Beaver dancing on broken glass in the playground was beside the point; everyone knew *Leave It to Beaver* wasn't real.

Camden is the product of a thought process that has reached its terminal point. The Breaker thought process gave us feudalism, industrialism, corporatism—and Camdenism. If you plant a kernel of corn, after a while you'll get a plant with big, fat ears of corn. If you plant the Breaker story of we–can–grow–forever industrialism and wait, you will get Camden.

At seventeen, I was an oddball. I was not a father. The result of "babies having babies" is that in a city of eighty thousand, over 50 percent of the population is under twenty years old. Forty-something great-grandparents are not uncommon.

Camden is not an accident. Camden was quite deliberately planted and cultivated. At the dawn of the twentieth century, the city was a Breaker success story, the shining buckle on the Industrial Belt, with the highest per capita income in the nation. Everyone had a job, the factories paid well, and never mind that brown haze that daily hung like a dirty veil over the streets. In the 1940s, the city was still living in the lap of prosperity.

Question: What happened over the last fifty years to reduce Camden to its present woeful state? Answer: Nothing. Camden's precipitous fall is the natural consequence of its soaring flight. In the general decline of Breaker society, Camden is an early-impact crater.

> When I was twelve or thirteen, I started drinking regularly. I progressed from a few sips of my mother's beer or mixed drinks to several bottles of beer a day, and then to the rot-gut wine with names like Tiger Rose and Thunderbird in dusty flat bottles with screw caps. I drank until my hair turned gray and fell out. I drank until I got lines all over my face. I drank until I looked older as a teenager than I do now, thirty years later. I drank to try to feed the hunger. It didn't work.
>
> There's nothing like pissing blood to get your attention that something's wrong. The wine had eaten the lining out of my stomach. I made a switch from alcohol to drugs, which treat the stomach more gently. It's been said that alcohol and drugs are the mystical experiences of the ignorant. To this I can attest.

Camden is a metaphor for the advanced decay of an overly urbanized environment, the price we pay for thinking that our actions against Nature and against each other do not have consequences.

> I carried a straight razor to high school. Guns weren't that popular back then and were really expensive. Everyone carried knives.

Switchblades were really popular, followed by the "box cutter," the single-edge razor blade that you can buy in a hardware store. The latter wasn't nearly as high status or impressive as the switchblade, but it had the advantage of legality.

My weapon of choice, a bone-handled straight razor, made a switchblade look downright pedestrian. Switchblades are clunky; a straight razor is elegant, refined, a precision instrument. Even opening it required finesse: any dummy could push a button, but it took artistry (and practice) to open a straight razor with one hand, without slicing off a few fingers in the process. However, its chief advantage from my point of view was that it was free: my uncle was a barber.

Like all other parts of The Mess, Camden does not have a solution that lies within the Breaker story, the consciousness that created it in the first place. Even the best and the brightest, swarming out of our colleges and universities like bumblebees out of the hive on a warm day, have not the faintest glimmer of what to do about Camden.

Some otherwise bright person got the idea of putting mini-parks on the vacant lots in some of Camden's troubled neighborhoods. Financed with federal funds, they are designed to be user friendly, with benches, built-in chess and checkers boards, sandlots, other urban amenities. They are really nice. Since they are padlocked, surrounded with ten-foot chain-link fences with barbed wire at the top, they probably will stay nice. No one can use them.

The State of New Jersey, the federal government, various foundations, all the king's horses and all the king's men can't seem to get this ugly, gooey mess back into its shell.

When the state sank millions into the waterfront Aquarium and adjoining park for Camden, they added a marina for about fifty midsize yachts. They were surprised to see the marina unused. They seemed not to know you really can't buy a yacht with food stamps.

Camden is not a problem. Camden is the *result* of a problem. It is the natural conclusion of the Breaker story that created industrialism and unrestricted growth.

Camden is what a society gets when it values money over people. Camden is not a failure of the system. Camden is the system in operation. It is the toxic fruit of a poisoned tree. Wherever Breaker society is going, Camden has gotten there first.

Camden is a social/political landfill, a dumping ground for society's unwanted spare parts. Camden exists because you think that you are in some way separate from it. We are taught that we are separated from the pain of others. Camden comes into being when I can dissociate my progress from your pain.

At fifteen or sixteen, I found a live baby in a trash can. Some girl had hidden her pregnancy from her parents, delivered her baby into a trash bag, and disposed of it in the alley. Babies in trash cans were fairly common; finding one still alive and kicking was not. We called the police, who took the baby away. If he's still alive, he's about thirty years old now. I sometimes wonder if rescuing the baby did him, or the world, a favor.

We think that by moving a few miles away to the middle-class sameness of the suburbs, we can avoid the horrors of Camden. We even delude ourselves into thinking that we are immune to those horrors.

Children of Rio

In Rio, as in many other Third World cities, life has become so hellish that thousands of children literally live on the streets, parentless.

Their parents may have died, may have abandoned them, may be drug-addicted or otherwise incapacitated.

The only way to describe the children is "feral." To say they are human is stretching the term. The children live quite literally on the street. They sleep in alleys and "hunt" in packs. The way they survive is to run into a store and eat as much food from the shelves as they possibly can before the store manager can grab them and throw them out. They go on to the next store and the next, repeating the action until they are satisfied. They do this every day; it is the only way they can obtain food. Like trying to sweep back the tide with a broom, the store owners fight a losing battle with the same children day after day. There is nothing the owners can do except kick them out.

Well, almost nothing. The shopkeepers and the police have come up with a "street solution": a bullet in the brain. Scores of Rio street kids have been found in alleyways, shot to death at close range. The worldwide outrage at this has been slow to build, since everyone recognizes that, within a system of exclusivity, other options are scarce. Death may be a mercy for a child who has no future beyond mere bodily survival. Murder is the societal solution to this problem.

(When a friend heard the story of Rio's children, he remarked that in America we are more efficient: we just sell our kids the guns and let them kill each other.)

Children of Portland

In Portland, Oregon, there is a shopping center, the Lloyd Center Mall, that caters to the moderately upscale. Being on Portland's East Side, it is the stepchild of the more fashionable City Center area, and is within easy access of Portland's ethnic neighborhoods.

A few years ago, a young man was innocently walking through the Lloyd Center with his girlfriend. Three teenagers came up on him and beat him so severely that pieces of his skull had to be removed from his brain. He will never be able to walk or speak as before. He had done nothing to provoke the attack. Though the surface issue was race, the real issue was spiritual starvation. The attackers were spiritually starved.

You will note this story does not state the race of the victim or the attackers. It is irrelevant. In the Breaker society, these roles switch and overlap constantly, creating a seamless web, a dance of violence, brutality, and cruelty. Did you attribute ethnicity to either attackers or victim? If so, how did you come to your conclusions? Now switch the ethnicities in your mind—does that change how you see this violent act?

Children of Affluence

Lest you believe that spiritual starvation is the by-product of race and poverty, let me present a nightmare about the children of affluence. From 1992 to 1994, I was on the core faculty of the Oregon Governor's School for Citizen Leadership (OGS), an annual leadership intensive for sixty students selected from around the state. The students were predominantly white and middle-class.

One of the exercises we would conduct with them was "Stand Up If . . ." On a purely voluntary basis, participants were asked to stand up if certain statements were true of them. Among the items was "Stand up if you have either attempted or seriously contemplated suicide."

Consistently, 60 percent of the students would stand up. They wanted to kill themselves. Why would these mostly middle-class kids attempt or consider suicide? As children of material affluence, they have been told that they have everything this society can provide. But they are still hungry. So they incorrectly surmise that something must be terribly wrong with *them*. Or they choose to leave a society that seems to have nothing else to offer. The net result: an incredibly high suicide rate.

We are taught to see suicide as an individual tragedy, a personal issue. In reality, suicide is political. Suicide is an extreme vote of no confidence in a society that doesn't work. Suicide is radical opting out. We have created a society our children want to leave. They want connection and instead get materiality. They want meaning and instead get a life devoid of cultural and spiritual richness, a life ripped free of context—historical, social, spiritual, communal. Breaker society acts as though neither The Mess nor the internal hunger gnawing at our youth is real.

The OGS students are fairly representative of average teenagers. America's middle-class children face spiritual starvation on a mass scale.

The Super-Rich and Ultra-Poor

My mother would have gone to prison if the State of New Jersey knew what she did to keep us alive. "Rent parties" in public housing—where food and drink are served to neighbors for the purpose of raising money for rent—are illegal, although sleeping on the streets with your children is not. Scrubbing floors or taking care of someone else's children while receiving a welfare check is illegal, although having your children malnourished or starving is not.

My mother, like tens of thousands of other women on welfare, was forced every year to raise a family on the amount of money that Michael Eisner, CEO of the Walt Disney Company, earns in *ten seconds.* ("Earns" is not exactly the right term, since no one person's time and talents are worth the hundreds of millions of dollars the Disney board of directors appropriates for him every year.) When Mr. Eisner goes to the bathroom to urinate, the amount of money he collects from Disney while emptying his bladder equals what a migrant farmworker struggling in the fields of California or Oregon earns in five years. And in the feeding frenzy at the pinnacles of global corporatism, Mr. Eisner is not the highest paid.

Children of the Forest

A redwood, with a lifespan of two thousand years or more, must have a different view of life from the one we have. A tree has a different rhythm, one closer to geologic time than ours. From a redwood's perspective, we are like mayflies, who are born, grow, evolve, mate, and die in a single day. We think that the tree is not conscious, only because we cannot begin to comprehend its consciousness.

We end that consciousness in a few human minutes with a chainsaw, without a thought of the unspeakable majesty that we have just terminated, without a thought of the grievous sin that we are committing. We are sad when a virus kills a human, but to the redwood, we are the virus. (This does not mean trees should not be cut, any more than broccoli should not be cut for my dinner. Life feeds on life. In order for me to "live," something has to "die." The issue is not whether a life is taken but whether a person is conscious of the sacredness of that life.)

The Soldier's Lottery

> In Sierra Leone, a country fractured by near-constant violent upheaval, the soldiers of a particular warlord round up the local villagers for a lottery. One by one, the villagers are forced to select a card. On the cards are drawings of various body parts: hands, feet, legs, arms, lips, and eyelids. The soldiers will cut off whatever body part is depicted on the villager's card. A few of the cards are blank; they entitle the villagers that draw them to walk away from the carnage.

The lottery is not played to terrorize or to punish. It is not played to coerce behavior from the villagers. It is simply the West African version of the "Coat Job" I performed in junior high school.

I have offered here a sampling of our era's nightmares, each a sobering witness to The Mess. But you could, without effort, come up with your own selection of nightmare stories. Pause for a few moments and think what they would be. What is your story concerning poverty and affluence? Your story involving children? Your story about the environment? Your story of hatred and violence?

Hold all these images in your mind and heart as you continue reading. These are not really separate horror stories but aspects of the same story. What will it take, short of a revolution, to change these images? What story is big enough to hold the solution to all of these problems? Remember: the problem is not The Mess; the problem is the consciousness that creates The Mess. The solution, therefore, must be an alternative state of consciousness.

A Soul-Starved Society

Our humanity has been violated. We are powerful spiritual beings living in a system that robs us of our power. We are sacred creatures in a desecrated land. We are not only hemmed in, we hem in each other. No wonder we act crazy.

We are starved. We live in a society that starves our souls. That starvation has led to a condition in which it is difficult to be fed, because we do not even know that there is something missing, that there is a necessary element to complete us.

Corporations use the words and symbols of spirituality, sacredness, and transcendence to sell overpriced cars and flavored water. And in a society that has lost its spiritual roots, it works.

Part of your spiritual starvation lies in being unreconciled to what you are. The Breaker consciousness teaches us to be dissatisfied with who and what we are, to aspire to be someone else, anyone else. You may be dissatisfied with being a man, being a woman, being a person of color, being six feet tall, having freckles, being "too old" or "too fat," having some condition that you cannot identify but feels *wrong*. We are taught to aspire to be the most alluring fashion model, the hottest movie star, the richest man or woman, the happy people in the commercials, anyone but ourselves.

If you feel this way, you can take some comfort in the fact that nearly everybody else feels this way also. As a friend said, "When I was in high school, all the girls hated how they looked and acted. Everyone wanted to be a cheerleader. Cheerleaders were the most popular, the sexiest, they had it all. Then, when I grew up, I realized that the former cheerleaders were some of the most miserable girls. They also hated how they looked and acted, but had nothing to aspire to!"

When I am not satisfied with *me*, I get angry at others.

> *Your [negative feeling] has little to do with the other person. It emerges from the discontent with the reality of your own life. [The negative feeling] is not a feeling directed toward others; it is a feeling directed against yourself. The feeling arises when you are not reconciled to the fact of what you are.*
>
> —VIMALA THAKAR[11]

In *Ishmael,* a paradigm-shifting novel by Daniel Quinn, a teacher speaks poetically of spiritual starvation among animals caged in a zoo:

> *In such places . . . where animals are simply penned up, they are almost always more thoughtful than their cousins in the wild. This is because even the dimmest of them cannot help but sense that something is very wrong with this style of living. . . . The tiger you see madly pacing its cage is . . . preoccupied with something that a human would certainly recognize as a thought. And this thought is a question: WHY? "Why, why, why, why, why?" the tiger asks itself hour after hour, day after day, year after year, as it treads its endless path behind the bars of its cage. It cannot analyze the*

*question or elaborate on it. If you were somehow able to ask the
creature, "Why what?" it would be unable to answer you. Nevertheless this question burns like an unquenchable flame in its
mind, inflicting a searing pain that does not diminish until the
creature lapses into a final lethargy that zookeepers recognize as
an irreversible rejection of life. And of course this questioning is
something that no tiger does in its normal habitat.*[12]

We can see people, young and old, hovering on the street
corners of our inner cities, immobilized like the leaf-cutter ants
who lost their queen. We see them roaming the walkways of the
regional malls. We see them wandering aimlessly in the play-
grounds of the rich. They are looking, just looking. Looking for
what? Is the tiger's question formed deep within them? Are they
asking themselves, "WHY?"

That was my internal question three decades ago. At the deepest core of my being, before I even had a language, I knew there
was something fundamentally wrong with my world picture. Of
course, I had no other pictures with which to compare it. Worst of
all, everyone else around me—my mother, my friends, my teachers—was acting as though the madness was *normal.*

Suppose someone were to ask you, "What's wrong here? What
can I do to help you?" how would you respond? If you are experiencing spiritual starvation, you cannot begin to answer that question, so you respond with easy formulas. The *6 O'clock News* sends
camera crews into the ghetto to cover the latest gang-related
shooting. They interview residents, who say the reasons for the
shooting include lack of jobs and poor housing. No one speaks (or
asks) about spiritual starvation.

Mislabeling Our Hunger

The Breaker society has starved our souls. We're hungry for what
we don't know and haven't experienced.

There's a hole, an empty place in my heart. I feel bad about it. I want it to go away. Someone tells me that the reason for my feelings of emptiness is something called "racism"; if we fixed this "racism," the emptiness would go away. Although the racism is real, the diagnosis is false.

> When I was twelve years old, a man named Malcolm X articulated the reason why the world did not work for black people though it worked for whites: the reason was racism. The argument made compelling sense to me and to lots of others in my virtually all-black community. Because we had little contact with or interest in the wider world where the racism theory might have been tested, we had no reason to doubt it.
>
> So for years I struggled to get the world to work for black people. Through demonstrations and protests, through economic and cultural development, through giving and receiving education, I struggled to make the world work—for the black community. Following the theory of black nationalism, I joined with others in attempting to create separate political, social, and economic institutions, ones that would be by and for African-Americans.
>
> In college I began to realize that my world view was incomplete: I saw that the world did not work for some white people, too. My struggle then expanded to include poor people of all ethnicities.
>
> The next shock came in realizing that the world did not work for some middle-class people also!
>
> Since that time, my world view has been constantly expanding, and I am now aware that the world does not work for anyone, whether human or nonhuman. The ultimate questions are not about race/ethnicity, poverty/affluence, political party or any other division of the world in the Breaker scheme of things. My ultimate question is this: In a world of

six billion humans and countless other beings, how can we create circumstances wherein each being can flourish, without limiting the life expression of others? In short, how can we create a world that truly works for all?

Racism did not cause my emptiness, and eliminating racism won't make it go away. My emptiness is the *same* as that of the white woman of affluence, the middle-class male, the people who blew up U.S. federal buildings in Oklahoma and East Africa, and tens of millions of others. The only difference is in the presenting symptoms.

This does *not* mean that racism (any more than our other "isms") doesn't exist. Racism is alive and well in our society. However, racism is just one form of exclusivity: "I am separate—by virtue of my skin color." If we could wave a magic wand and make racism disappear, we would still be left with countless other ways to practice exclusivity. The notion "I am separate" is the root of all our problems, including some for which we don't yet have names.

While racism feeds my emptiness, my feelings of separation and rejection, it in turn is fed by the emptiness and delusions of separation of others. Spiritual starvation maintains the vicious circle.

Feeding Our Hunger

We know how to feed physical hunger, but not emotional, social, and spiritual hungers. We learned as newborns that if we opened our mouth and yelled, someone would put a bottle or a breast in it, and we would get full. Simple and repeatable. Except that sometimes when we opened our mouth and yelled, we were looking for something else, and had no way of articulating it. Even when we acquire a spoken language, we cannot articulate our inner hunger. Those who taught us to speak had never been taught how to express *their* hunger. So we search for satisfaction through work, through relationships, through material possessions, and still stay unfed.

Tragically, the unsatisfied spiritual hunger of parents is often blatant in the condition of their children.

THE SINS OF THE PARENTS

A couple of years ago, on a rare bright fall day in Portland, I was on a bus when the third and fourth graders from Irvington Elementary School got on. All of a sudden, I was surrounded by little ones. There was a mad scramble for seats, with children jockeying for position, squealing, "I want Holly to sit next to me!" "Jane, come sit with us!"

However, there were two students no one called to, no one wanted to sit next to. One came and sat by me, the other sat by herself.

The child who sat next to me smelled of stale urine. Her matted hair had not been combed for days. It was obvious from the dried-riverbed look of her skin that she had not had a bath in weeks. Although the weather was cool, she was the only child who was not wearing a coat; she had on a battered adult sweater that perhaps her teacher had found for her.

The reason none of the children wanted to sit next to her was not her race. Almost every white student on the bus was sitting with a student of color; and the African-American students were among the most popular in the group.

The student sitting next to me was shunned because she stank and was dirty. There is no label to describe this child's condition, or the state of emptiness of her parents. Both the child and her parents were suffering from spiritual starvation. If you had told her mother that none of the other children wanted to sit next to her child, she would no doubt have retorted, "They're probably a bunch of racists."

The Quest for "More"

Do you experience spiritual starvation in your relationship? You may have a partner who gives you everything you ask for and need, is responsive to you in every way . . . yet you still feel empty. There is still a voice inside of you that says you haven't been fed yet. And you may have been acculturated to believe that your emptiness is due to the fact that you aren't getting enough from your mate, even though you get *everything*.

If you don't have much money, you may falsely believe that your emptiness is caused by poverty and that the cure is getting "enough money." This is especially true if everyone who has money looks as though they're having more fun than you. Author and counselor Emmet Fox once stated that he would rather counsel rich people than poor people, since rich people already know that money will not solve their problems.

A person with an ample reserve of dollars can still experience the hunger. What would drive someone to work long, hard hours to make his second billion? Or his seventh? What drives a person to reach for more when she already has more than enough? It is up to each person to judge for himself or herself how much is "enough" to sustain an acceptable life. However, it is safe to say that someone with $7 billion—more money than can effectively be spent in seven lifetimes—who is still working hard to increase his holdings is having a problem with money addiction. An analogy: though it is not my intention to pass judgment on how people choose to drink alcohol, if someone tells me that they drink seven fifths of liquor per day, I would refer them to a hospital or clinic. It is interesting that money is our most socially acceptable addiction: I know of no clinics that treat people addicted to money. (Gambling clinics treat people for *squandering* their money.)

The late billionaire real estate developer James Rouse and the millionaire actor Paul Newman come to mind as examples of people who love making money—and love giving it away just as fast as they make it. Rouse poured his wealth into the Enterprise Foundation, which teaches poor people how to build their own housing. All profits from the "Newman's Own" brand of gourmet foods are given to charity. Knowing how much is enough allows this to happen.

The quest to fill our emptiness by acquiring more material things drives our economy and our social and cultural industries, as well as our stress disorders, our neuroses, and our depressions.

The belief that money will cure the emptiness keeps many of us locked into the acquisition game that lies near the heart of Breaker society. The myth is that once you get enough "things"—a big enough paycheck or car or home—you will no longer feel empty.

This *never* happens. Money and material possessions never fill the gap. We should draw a lesson from the gerbil's exercise wheel: it goes around and around, lots of energy is expended, but the gerbil gets nowhere.

The Consensual Lie: "We're Okay"

We live in a society that perpetuates a great lie: that our social institutions, our communities, our lifestyles, our relationships with the environment, our shared world view are basically okay, even desirable. The Breaker story is okay. Exclusivity is okay. We are told that a world that practices exclusivity is a desirable world. Everyone else wants to be like us, which is good.

Our official social myth is an illusion. For most of us, it is not "Morning in America," Ronald Reagan's version of the Breaker story. We pretend to believe in this lie. We teach it to our children. We do this because the alternative is to admit that something is very wrong.

At some level, we know that everything is far from okay, that in fact we are alienated, disconnected, cut off from Nature, from other people, and from ourselves. Deep inside, we know that we are poisoning our environment, poisoning our bodies, poisoning our spirit. Such pervasive disconnection leaves us with an inarticulate emptiness of the soul. Rather than face that emptiness, we participate in the lie. If we are to be really truthful, we have to face our emptiness. But we get really angry at people who ask us to do so.

Examples of the Consensual Lie

- We buy the loaf of bread that has a picture of a quaint old-time family harvesting wheat and baking bread by hand. That picture is a lie. *We all know it's a lie.* Everyone knows that the bread in the wrapper is a mixture of chemicals produced in a factory. However, we cannot tell ourselves the truth about the bread because we would have to admit that we are eating machine-made food.
- Advertisers would have us believe that everyone who smokes cigarettes is immensely happy, and really good-looking. You would think that tobacco was a combination of marijuana and a powerful aphrodisiac. This image is a lie. Go look at the people pulling around oxygen tanks, wheezing through cigarette-damaged lungs, or trying to talk with a tracheal hole from cancer-related surgery—do they look happy or sexy?
- We are prompted to buy a car by the commercial that shows the car whizzing down a beautiful leaf-strewn country road at ninety miles an hour. This is a lie: we will never drive that car in such conditions. The commercial promises something that will never be delivered.
- As of this writing, the U.S. government is congratulating itself that domestic unemployment is at an all-time low. This is a lie. The ranks of the perpetually unemployed have never been higher—it's just that these unemployed are not counted in the total.[13] People's lives get worse, even as the statistics get better.
- Once every four years, many of us participate in a political charade. We pretend that the Breaker society will change

because of a beauty contest that installs a new personality in an overly large residence in Washington, D.C. We know that this exercise is a lie, a pretense. And we acquiesce in the pretense. Political ritual replaces political life. It is self-indulgent, self-promoting, and basically pointless. Congress spends time investigating itself and the sins of past and current administrations. The courts undo the latest legislation. The government spends more and more money to do less and less.

These and many, many other public lies are told and reaffirmed as a mask for our emptiness. We lie because we cannot face the magnitude of The Mess. We consent because it's easier than curing our emptiness. The consensual lie is practiced so constantly in our society that we begin to think that telling the truth is wrong.

When my eldest daughter was in fifth or sixth grade, she asked me a homework question: "What is the principal cash crop in Florida?"

My answer was immediate. I didn't even look up from my newspaper. "Marijuana."

The next day, her teacher sent a note home, asking for a conference. At the conference, I supplied the teacher with statistics that conservatively estimated the marijuana crop at twice the value of citrus products. She said, "That may be true, but it's not the answer we want. It's too controversial."

I declined her invitation to participate in the consensual lie. I told her that I expected my daughter to get an "A" unless the teacher presented hard evidence refuting my assertion or redefined the question. My daughter got her "A."

The teacher expected us to participate in the lie that our economy is not based on drugs, pornography, stealing, or other activities we label criminal or antisocial. By our refusal to consent, the teacher had to face her own acquiescence in the lie. What was she teaching her students about society? Why was it important to lie to them?

THE GREENGROCER

There is a story in Václav Havel's seminal essay "The Power of the Powerless" about a greengrocer. The greengrocer is asked by a local party boss to put a sign in the window: "Workers of the World Unite!" The grocer does so, not because he believes in the slogan, nor because he is afraid. He complies because he may get better vegetables in the next shipment. And why not? Everyone else is doing it.

A secretary passes by and sees his sign. She has one on her desk, too. Not because she believes it, nor because she is afraid, but because she may get a raise faster if she complies. And anyway, everyone else is doing it.

The local deputy party boss who is passing out the signs does so not because he believes the slogan, nor because he is afraid, but because he wants to be party boss one day. And anyway, everyone else is doing it.[14]

The secretary and the greengrocer reinforce each other's participation in the lie. Without knowing each other, they each make it easier for the other to participate in the lie. Both are "powerless," yet they actively help to sustain the system that robs them of their power.

THE THIEVES' MARKET

In Charlotte, North Carolina, as in any major city, there are places where thieves go to sell their goods. One impromptu market is at a gas station on Beatties Ford Road, a main artery running through the black community. On almost any Saturday morning, the sellers park in a certain spot, open their trunks, and, keeping a watchful (but largely unnecessary) eye out for the police, make their sales.

On one occasion, while buying gas, I noticed among the market's shoppers someone who looked familiar. It was an acquaintance, Reverend "Smith," a local minister. Mistaking my presence for acceptance, he joked about picking up some suits "at a discount." After letting him know that I was buying gas and did not approve of the market, he offered a string of justifications and explanations, ranging from his "poverty" to the "cultural norm" of buying stolen goods.

I refused to consent to the lie that it is okay to shop at the Thieves' Market. In reality, Reverend Smith and those who shopped alongside him created this market, just as much as the people who actually removed the goods from the shelves. No one would spend their Saturdays standing over the open trunk of their car unless there were buyers. Reverend Smith, whether he recognized the fact or not, was a sponsor of larceny.

The Four Symptoms of Spiritual Starvation

There are any number of ways in which our spiritual starvation manifests itself in our daily lives. Here we will focus briefly on four key symptoms: anger and violence; escapist behavior; denial and numbing; and control and manipulation.

Anger and Violence

Anger can be an appropriate, healthy, and even necessary reaction to an outrageous or unacceptable condition. Being stuck in anger, however, is neither appropriate nor healthy. The constant expression of anger is really the expression of our emptiness.

Many times, we don't know why we're angry, or what we are really angry about. Recently, I was awakened by loud cursing across the street from my house. Apparently, a car had turned the corner too close to the sidewalk and a pedestrian had had to jump back. For five long minutes, this man stood cursing the driver, who of course was nowhere to be seen. Clearly he was very angry, but it seemed to me his anger had nothing to do with the traffic incident. This kind of reflex anger usually has its roots in general feelings of powerlessness, a nameless rage at the confines of an invisible prison. Something about the car incident reminded the man that he was indeed powerless.

A friend related a fender bender incident in which four young men jumped from the struck car, brandishing guns. Is a dented fender worth taking someone's life? The source of that anger must lie elsewhere.

What is the urban underclass angry about? Does it really have anything to do with a police shooting, or whether someone like Rodney King is beaten? These triggering events are fairly arbitrary; it is the ambient conditions that are more significant. This doesn't mean that the participants in urban insurrection are not angry about the Rodney King of that day; it just means that the triggering event is only that—something that sparks an explosion long in the making.

What are middle-class Americans angry about? Is it really about whether or not someone gets a few hundred dollars in welfare payments? No. Although the triggering events among whites and blacks are very different, the underlying causes are the same: anger at a society that doesn't make sense; rage and despair over a deep sense of powerlessness.

If our anger does not have a convenient label, we will invent one. For example, if I am black and feel disaffected, I will label my anger "black rage" (which nowadays is politically correct). This obscures the fact that virtually all crimes committed in the black community are perpetrated against other black people. "Black rage" aimed at other blacks has no name, is not politically correct, yet is exactly the same terrifying experience for the victims as rage directed at whites. If Rodney King had not been beaten by the police, chances are he would have been assaulted by those who protested his beating.

If I am white and feel disaffected, I will label my anger "white backlash," cut my hair and go looking for some people of color or some gays to stomp. If I am middle-class, the "stomping" may come in the form of legislation or lawsuits against affirmative action.

In this society, we act out our spiritual starvation by engaging in destructive behavior against ourselves or others. Women, because of the way they are socialized, tend to exhibit destructive behavior toward themselves. We label these behaviors "anorexia," "bulimia," "self-mutilation," "suicide," "drug abuse." The way men are socialized leads them to act destructively toward others. We label their behaviors "homicide," "rape," "senseless violence," "hate crimes." Same violent impulses, different expressions.

Escapist Behavior

What do we get out of beating someone, or vandalizing property, or rape, or verbal attack? I can say from personal knowledge that putting a brick through a plate-glass window is incredibly *releasing*. For a few moments after I did it, I felt powerful, in control, in the spotlight, no longer invisible. This is typical of releasing/ escapist behavior. The perpetrator forgets for a moment that he is powerless. But because escapist behavior is largely illusory, it has to be repeated.

Two illegal but prevalent forms of release/escape are drug abuse (including abuse of prescription drugs) and violence (from spousal battery to rape). Legally acceptable forms of release/escape include alcohol consumption, impulse shopping, joy riding, "sport sex" and pornography, and sanctioned violence (contact sports, hunting). "Road rage" also belongs in this category. When you last yelled and cursed at someone who cut in front of you in traffic, did you not have a momentary feeling of release?

My friends who practice bulimia tell me that they feel a sense of power and control when eating and purging. They're released from their subjective state of helplessness.

A graffiti artist experiences release when reducing a $10,000 billboard to meaningless gibberish or imposing on it a powerful countermessage.

How would it feel to blow up a multistory building? What feelings of power would that generate?

We are staring into the dark mirror of spiritual starvation, where all of the above acts serve a similar psychological purpose. We confuse release and fulfillment, because we do not know what fulfillment is. We do not know how to feed our hunger.

Sadly, temporary release merely maintains spiritual starvation. Sending a brick through a window, pushing a car off the edge of a cliff, beating someone up, raping someone may provide a tremendous sense of relief from the ache of starvation, but the respite is brief and the need to repeat the act becomes overwhelming.

The primary economy of America is the Economy of Temporary Release. Cars, after-shave, beer, and almost everything else are all sold on the premise that they will release you from your hunger, feed your starved spiritual body. It's all a part of the Consensual Lie.

The economics of legal and illegal forms of escapist/release behaviors flow together. We cannot truly wage war on drugs without first acknowledging the benefits we all receive from the multibillion-dollar drug trade. We cannot fight prostitution or pornography without first understanding how we use sex to sell everything.

Denial and Numbing

Another way in which spiritual starvation manifests itself is through denial and numbing.

We have seen pictures of children who are starved for food—the vacant, lost look in the eyes, the numb expressions, the lack of reaction, even when food is presented to them. Compare this to the average American child (and many an adult) lost in front of a television.

Going numb is a typical response to painful stimuli. Going emotionally numb means turning off one's responsiveness to emotional events. The numb person needs a really big kick to know that he feels anything at all.

Control and Manipulation

Ultimately, we try to fill our emptiness by attempting to control and manipulate our world. This is the impetus behind our ever increasing efforts to subjugate the more-than-human environment, to punish and constrain other people's behavior, and to stifle and regiment ourselves.

Control never succeeds in satisfying the hunger within. Even Breakers know this. However, Breakers convince each other that controlling hasn't worked because it wasn't perfect enough. With just a little more control, things will be better . . .

Receptivity to Love

The Love Paradox: "We all just need to love each other" is both truth and crap. If you are *unable* to give or receive love, the above statement is as good as an instruction to a blind person that she should become more aware of color.

Yusef is dying. A five-year-old boy, he is down to only a few pounds in weight, and his face has the glassy stare of one who sees into his own death. He is dying from a completely curable malady.

When I visited Uganda in late 1993, I learned that, although Uganda is the AIDS capital of the world, the leading cause of death in that country is diarrhea and other common childhood maladies. Yusef is dying from what in the West would be a relatively minor complaint. The problem with diarrhea is that the child quickly loses the capacity to absorb water. Even if Yusef, and the millions of Ugandan children like him, had access to plenty of clean water, it would just go in one end and out the other. A medical doctor told me that giving a child water under these circumstances could hasten his death, since the water washes away nutrients more quickly.

There is only one way to help Yusef: teach his body to absorb water again. This is done by introducing very inexpensive chemicals to his drinking water by means of an "oral rehydration packet." Similarly, the only way to help someone who is spiritually starved is to teach him or her how to absorb love, how to absorb the sacred, perhaps for the first time.

The Buddha said, "We learn not from experience but from our *capacity* to experience." What happens if we never developed the capacity to experience love, fulfillment, the sacred? What if our parents never passed on to us the vital information necessary for our survival as whole beings?

If a person is suffering spiritual "dehydration," it is not that potentially fulfilling events do not happen in her life; it is that she lacks the capacity to absorb the experiences that do occur. Someone can tell her that she is beautiful or that she is loved, but she will still have no *experience* of being beautiful or loved. She may command abundant resources but still experience poverty.

How do we connect with those who suffer, in the words of Albert Einstein, the "delusions of separation"? How do we help the starving among us absorb love?

The Spiritual Rehydration Packet

For millions of people, the various Twelve Step programs, derived from the highly successful prototype Alcoholics Anonymous, have been a "spiritual rehydration packet." The Twelve Step approach is particularly helpful when a person is trying to overcome a specific negative or addictive pattern in his or her life.

For me, the process of absorbing love has been one of reminding myself that I am *receiving* love. Constantly. When I am focused on the emptiness, it seems that I am the only person in the world who is not receiving love. God loves everyone but me. My starvation means that my emotional and spiritual bodies are not absorbing the love that I'm receiving.

Yusef's recovery means that his body starts to absorb the water he is given. My recovery? My emotional and spiritual bodies begin to absorb the love that is flowing around me constantly. Simply acknowledging that I am receiving love helps me to become more open to it.

I look for ways I can share love with others. In giving love to others, I act "as if" I am full of love. This reinforces my awareness of receiving love.

My spiritual rehydration packet involves reconnecting—with myself, with others, with the more-than-human environment, with the Spirit. As we will see in greater detail in Chapter 7, these connections are ever-present and are hard-wired into our systems. We ignore these important connections at our peril.

Once we have addressed our spiritual starvation, we can begin the practice of inclusivity.

3

INCLUSIVITY—
SPIRIT AND PRACTICE

Work as Spiritual Practice

MY WORK IS my spiritual path, a spiritual calling dressed in the language of the practical. I don't wear special robes, speak in foreign tongues, or have a solemn expression. Lord knows I'm not celibate.

Like any path, at times its course is clear for miles ahead, and at other times it takes a sharp curve around a bend and I have to work hard not to wind up in a ditch. There are times when my work elevates me to heights of ecstasy. Generally, these are not the times when the fax machine gets stuck, the phone rings incessantly, and yet another report is due. Whether elevation or excavation, it's still my path.

My work is my spiritual practice, and Commonway Institute is my principal vehicle for that practice. The institute's focus is *inclusivity*—teaching the theory, philosophy, and practice of the inextricable linkage between our individual lives and The Other. The links already exist; we just help people become conscious of them. We conduct classes and projects that bring people together across the boundaries that seem to separate them. We humans have much more that unites us than separates us; Commonway helps people see that. We encourage people to see what they have in common and to build on that common ground. We work with blue-collar workers and university professors, farmers and farm-workers, management and labor, and many more who see themselves as being in conflict. We believe that this practice of inclusivity is the essence of virtually every spiritual tradition.

We are engaged in building community through collaborative, inclusive dialogue on fundamental issues affecting society. Through communication, people discover their hidden kinship. We believe that somewhere in the heartfelt communion of two or more souls the Spirit can be found. We encourage people to practice the essence of the spiritual teachings that have been given them, regardless of the source of their authority.

How can we walk into a room full of hostile, defended white males and find common ground? How can we go to a foreign country and help two traditionally warring parties listen to each other when their history, culture, and identity are deeply bound up in *not* listening to each other? How can we assist people in arriving at a new solution when they are firmly committed to their current solution, which involves killing The Other?

Inclusivity Is the Essence of Spirituality

The essence of an inclusive spiritual practice can be summed up in what Jesus is said to have called the second great commandment: "Thou shalt love thy neighbor as thyself." By "neighbors," Jesus did not mean merely those people who live close to us, but everyone with whom we have contact.

It's all well and good to say that we should love The Other, but how do we establish contact with those who want to distance themselves from us, ignore us, or even harm us? It's fine for Jesus to talk about loving our neighbors, but did he ever walk the streets of New York City, Washington, D.C., or our other large urban centers, where people flip you the finger at the slightest provocation? Where beggars curse you for not giving them money? Where nearly everyone carries a gun to protect himself from everyone else? How can we practice inclusivity in a world like this?

For example, in May of 1998, while in St. Petersburg, Russia, I was threatened by four skinheads while walking down the street. How could I practice "Love thy neighbor" when my "neighbors" were threatening to kill me?

There is a wonderful book that describes, in a very different context, the steps we can take to defuse such incidents, to build connection, community, and inclusivity. In *The Tibetan Book of Living and Dying*, Sogyal Rinpoche tells us how to connect authentically and communicate powerfully with those who are approaching death. Sogyal's practice with the dying can lead to better communication and greater spiritual connection with the living.

The Steps of Inclusivity

In this section, the words in bold at the head of each numbered section are from *The Tibetan Book of Living and Dying*.[15]

1. **The most essential thing in life is to establish an unafraid, heartfelt communication with others.**

We move forward on this path by not allowing our fear of The Other to prevent us from attempting to communicate.

Remember that the overwhelming majority of human communication is nonverbal. In my encounter with the Russian skinheads, I was in conscious communication with them from a half-block away. Every step I took, all of my eye contact, the look on my face, said to them: "I see you. I acknowledge your humanity. I know you are in pain, but I am not the cause of it and hurting me will not ease it. I am with you. Whatever you are feeling, I am feeling." In this conversation, we did not have to say a word. Although I said and did nothing, they backed off. (I was actually aided by the fact that I did not speak Russian and they apparently did not speak English. When one of them rushed me and started screaming at me, I did not react negatively, partly because I honestly had no idea what he was saying. I did not let the words get in the way of the communication.)

2. **The . . . essential thing is to relax any tension in the atmosphere in whatever way comes most easily and naturally. . . . Just be natural and relaxed, be yourself.**

When you think you are going to be hurt, either physically or emotionally, you get tense, your muscles lock, your jaw tightens, your eyes narrow. It is difficult to relax and be natural. The tension is produced by the "fight or flight" response, not by The Other, who may be oblivious to the situation:

- A driver locks his car doors and rolls up his windows when he sees a person of color approaching on the street. The person of color poses no threat to the driver, doesn't even see him.

- A woman walking down the street tenses and crosses the street to avoid an approaching man. The man isn't even aware of her.

Years ago, when leaving the Portland Public Library around sunset, I saw an elderly couple emerging from their car. The driver left the lights on. Although they were a little bit out of my way, I hurried down the steps and toward the couple. "Excuse me, sir!" I shouted from about forty feet away. Perhaps it was my imagination, but it appeared that they sped up their pace. I trotted a little closer, about ten feet. "Excuse me, sir!" No reaction. Perhaps they couldn't hear. I touched the man on the shoulder. He spun around quickly, a look of rage on his face. I pointed to his car. "You left your lights on." It took him a few seconds to realize he wasn't being mugged and that I was doing him a favor. To him, I was The Other. Though there was no threat, he was in a state of high tension.

Another story. This time, I am encountering The Other. An older black man walked into my office while I was conducting a meeting. Hand outstretched, he asked softly, "Do you have a quarter?" I quickly turned away from him, holding my hand up in the "halt" gesture. "We're busy." My unconscious avoidance reaction was typical of a class encounter.

Instead of retreating, he came closer and said, "I need a quarter." He stuck his hand in my face: in his palm were two dimes and five pennies.

To cover my embarrassment, I offered to give him the quarter. Again speaking softly, he said, "I don't need your charity, just your quarter."

It is the responsibility of the person experiencing the tension to try to dissolve it, without taking unnecessary risks with his or her personal safety. One of the most effective methods is to make eye contact and, if appropriate, smile—or at least look pleasant.

Smiling at the Russian skinheads was not appropriate, but making eye contact and looking pleasant was. In the face of the screaming, gesturing Russian, I stood my ground, made eye contact, tried to look unafraid and pleasant. He and his buddies backed down.

Into each life some pain, some aggravation, some unpleasantness comes. Author and Zen teacher Cheri Huber says, "Pain happens to all, suffering is your choice of what to do in the face of pain."[16] If you recognize that you cannot be truly hurt, you can relax into the moment.

If the skinheads were going to physically beat me, I was going to be beaten. "Fight or flight," running or attacking first, would have guaranteed a beating. Relaxing and easing the tension allowed other, less aggressive behaviors to come forward. Instead of fighting or fleeing, my preferred approach is to stay and engage.

In our Commonway work, we take steps to ensure a safe environment for dialogue. The atmosphere for a meeting should be as relaxed as possible for all parties. That requires that the coordinators and facilitators carefully choose a neutral location, that there be no offensive images or symbols present, and that the meeting itself not be allowed to get out of hand.

3. Encourage the person . . . to feel as free as possible to express thoughts, fears and emotions . . .

Fear comes in various flavors, like the ice cream in the freezer case at the store. You don't have to know the particular flavor to know that it's ice cream. Likewise, you do not have to know the flavor of the fear in order to know that fear is present.

In our projects, we assume that if someone is displaying anger, aggression, or violence, it is because he or she is afraid. Don't deal with the display, deal with the underlying fear. Encourage the person to acknowledge and give voice to the fear.

If a man is overtly angry, aggressive, or violent, it is because he does not have an outlet for expressing his underlying fears and uncertainties. He may be locked into seeing himself as powerless. He may have been taught that it is wrong or bad or weak to display one's fears. He may have been taught that violence is an appropriate response to unpleasantness. A million other things may block him from constructively expressing his fears.

Providing him with an expressive outlet can be a powerful way to short-circuit violence. In many instances, simply listening will open avenues for channeling fear and anger into constructive action.

4. [D]o not interrupt, deny, or diminish what the person is saying. . . . Learn to listen, and learn to receive in silence.

We cannot work with The Other when we are too filled with ourselves. We cannot listen because we are too busy preparing what we are going to say next.

In our project work, the hardest and most valuable part of the work is the least visible: listening. We conduct in-house exercises in active listening, then practice listening in every encounter, every workshop, every dialogue, every meeting.

When taking notes in a meeting, Commonway facilitators and coordinators are encouraged to divide their paper into three columns, headed

1. What the person is saying
2. What I want to say
3. What I think is currently going on in the room

This helps the facilitator to stay in touch with the entire unfolding situation. The facilitator sustains the listening attitude for everyone in the room.

Depending on the particular dynamics of a meeting, the facilitator will determine if the speaker should continue, when and how others should participate, and whether the speaker should be challenged. If the facilitator is truly listening, she will know the right thing to do.

5. **In all grave situations of life, two things are most useful: a common-sense approach and a sense of humor. . . . Use humor . . . as skillfully and as gently as possible.**

I can't imagine doing my work without telling lots of jokes and humorous anecdotes. It's a great way to break the ice in a room and to put yourself at the same level as the participants. (Most of my jokes are about my own past mistakes and gaffes.) Humor is also necessary to release the nervousness and tension that build up in a room when people are dealing with deep issues.

Most of our work deals with the deepest of people's fears about The Other. It is very difficult work—sometimes participants dissolve in tears or lash out at each other in shouting matches.

Without the application of common sense and humor, people could wind up in worse shape than when they started.

Common sense:

- A shouting match might be a good way for people to blow off steam—don't automatically stifle aggressive speech.
- An instant resolution of a long-standing conflict may not be feasible—allow the parties time to integrate what they are learning about themselves and each other.
- Stamina is not equally distributed—make sure that those with less staying power are not being exhausted by those with more.

6. **No one wishes to be "rescued" with someone else's beliefs. Remember your task is not to convert anyone to anything, but to help the person in front of you get in touch with his or her own strength, confidence, faith and spirituality, whatever that might be.**

One of the hardest things to do in our sessions is not to have an opinion. Our job is not to have the "answers" but to help those taking part arrive at their own solutions. We walk in the door not with a product but with a process.

When we start work in a new setting, most people ask us, with suspicion: "Why are you here? What's your agenda?" They are surprised, even incredulous, when we say: "We don't have an agenda. We don't care what you do, as long as all of you agree. Our job is to build community."

We start from a basic premise: the answers are in the group. We create processes that allow a group of people to arrive at their own answers, not adopt ours. Once they see that we are serious about not having an agenda, they find their own capacity to make the changes necessary for the good of all.

7. **Do not expect too much from yourself, or expect your help to produce miraculous results.**

I have had four "close encounters" with skinheads, two in the United States and two abroad. In each instance, I was able to apply the techniques I have been discussing and defuse the situation. However, before each incident, I said to myself, "It could be that you're about to get your ass kicked."

This acknowledgment provided a number of benefits:

- Release from the arrogant belief that my techniques can "make" The Other do anything.
- Acceptance of the fact that ass-kickings happen, and sometimes to people who simply don't deserve them. It might just be my time.
- Detachment from any sense of responsibility for the course of events. If the skinheads were to beat me, it would not be because I wasn't powerful enough, or did not correctly apply Technique No. 99.

8. For real communication to be established, you must make a determined effort to see the person in terms of his or her own life.

Why would a person beat up a total stranger? From the point of view of *your* life, this may seem like "senseless violence." From the point of view of *his* life, it makes all the sense in the world.

In a tragic high school shooting here in Oregon in 1998, a boy fired on his fellow classmates at random, using a high-powered rifle. He killed two and injured twenty-two others. He had already murdered both of his parents at home. To the shooter, taking these lives was a reasonable way to express his rage. He and other similarly troubled youth around the nation feel that such actions make sense.

It is impossible for me to understand a person's behavior unless I take on his perspective. And having done that, I might be able to help him find more creative and positive outlets for the energy surging within him.

9. Look at the . . . person in front of you and think of that
person as just like you, with
  • the same needs
  • the same fundamental desire to be happy and
    avoid suffering
  • the same loneliness
  • the same fear of the unknown
  • the same secret areas of sadness
  • the same half-acknowledged feelings of helplessness

**You will find that if you really do this, your heart will open
toward the person and love will be present between you.**

This really works. For decades, we demonized the Soviets as inhuman barbarians bent on world conquest and domination. They did the same to us. Now, we both realize that we are all human, with the same wants, needs, fears and joys. This was always true, but our fears hid our mutual interests and humanity.

The same thing is true with skinheads.

In our Commonway dialogue sessions, it is amazing to see people awakening to the fact that The Other is just like "us." When people start really listening to each other, and recognizing that they have the same needs and emotions, a powerful opportunity is created for inclusive community.

You think it might be asking too much for people to actually *love* each other? In the sense that they start hugging, kissing, and grinning, yes. But in the sense that they begin to feel concern for the well-being of The Other, no. We have seen this happen countless times in our meetings.

One example of many: A meeting was about to begin when
William said, "Let's not start until Pablo gets here." One year
earlier, William had tried to bar Pablo from the meetings. Now,
after working with him and seeing him as a human being instead

of The Other, William was concerned about Pablo's welfare and participation.

Put yourself directly and unflinchingly in the [other] person's place. . . . Really ask yourself
- **what would you most need?**
- **what would you most like?**
- **what would you really wish from the [person] in front of you?**

What did the four skinheads moving in on me need? The surface answer is that they needed to beat up a black guy walking down the street. I am sure they don't get many opportunities. But *why* would they need that? What would I need if our positions were reversed?

Our positions *have been* reversed: the "Coat Jobs" referred to in Chapter 2 were random beatings. In a world of brutal anonymity, the Coat Job was my attempt at becoming visible, at being *somebody*. Of course, at the time, this need was not conscious.

Making eye contact with the skinheads, not flinching from the encounter, was my way of saying: "I see you. You are somebody. I recognize your humanness." They got what they really needed. The beating was unnecessary.

10. **Don't try to be too wise; don't always try to search for something profound to say. You don't have to do or say anything to make things better. Just be there as fully as you can.**

The majority of our communications are nonverbal; we can help The Other be more relaxed and focused by being open and accepting. It may take a few times, but it is worth the effort.

Trying to be wise focuses on yourself. Focusing on others means you just have to show up and pay attention.

11. **[T]he person in front of me . . . is always, somewhere, inherently good. . . . Focusing on that inner goodness will**

give you the control and perspective you need to be as helpful as possible. . . . Treat [The Other] as if they were what they are sometimes capable of being: open, loving, and generous.

When we demonize The Other, we see all of her bad qualities and none of her good. There are no completely evil people. Nobody is purely bad, totally incapable of loving and being loved. Some of us may be so damaged that it is very difficult to express our love, but it is still there.

The Russian skinhead in front of me, a large young man, his face screwed up into a grimace of hatred, shouting at me from about three or four feet away, doesn't always look like this. When he pets his dog, he looks kind. When he's talking to his younger sister, he looks concerned. In fact, with his three other friends moments before he saw me, he was happily laughing. I focused on the friendly view of him.

As Breakers, we are taught to pay attention only to the negative aspects of The Other. "Those people" always act like that. *No one always acts like anything.*

If I believe I get attention or protection as a result of my negative behavior, I will present that behavior when encountering The Other. Most of us do this.

- A woman sees a man she finds interesting, yet adopts a "tough" attitude when he approaches.
- Two children circle each other warily on the playground before settling down to play.
- Strangers at a bar try to stare each other down.
- Two teenagers with hard expressions flash opposing gang hand signs at each other.

Therefore, our first encounter with The Other is usually the most difficult. If we can get beyond the surface behavior, we can find the place within each of us that is open, loving, and generous.

12. You cannot help [The Other] until you have acknow-
    ledged how their fear . . . disturbs you and brings up your
    most uncomfortable fears. Working with [The Other] is
    like facing a polished and fierce mirror of your own reality.

Ultimately, whatever we see in The Other is what exists in ourselves. If we pretend that we are comfortable with everyone and
that no one pushes our buttons, we are not honestly facing our
mirror. The Other helps us by encouraging us to face what we
most shrink from in ourselves.

Inclusivity: Moving Beyond Fear

Moving beyond fear may be the single most important thing that
you can do for yourself. And your planet.

Exclusivity is based in fear: fear that there will not be enough,
fear that The Other will hurt me in some way, fear of death, the
fear of any process outside of Breaker control.

Fear drove the arms race, which consumed trillions of dollars
in human and natural resources, drained the economies of all of
the countries engaged in it, and undermined the political, economic, and social structures of one of the competitors. The arms
race has no finish line and no winners. The U.S., still fearful, de-
signs new and more powerful nuclear weapons, although we
cannot identify an enemy against whom they will be used.

We fear death and spend billions of dollars each year on medical efforts to stave it off. But prolongation of life is often pursued
at the expense of the quality of that life.

Young people today have no experience of—and no expecta-
tion of ever living in—a society not based in fear. They hear stories about how in the past you could leave your car keys in the
ignition and never lock your doors. To them, such notions are as
quaint as horses and buggies, or three-cornered hats.

As someone said, moving beyond fear is simple—but not easy.
To move beyond fear, we simply decide to stop being afraid, or at

least to stop acting out of our fear. The notion that one can decide to stop *feeling* fear may strike some readers as hopelessly unrealistic, like asking a child dying of diarrhea to "decide" to be well. However, over time, we can build the confidence to take increasingly large steps in the direction of courage, community, and inclusivity. (In some of my work bringing people in conflict together, simply getting them to agree on the time for the next meeting is a major confidence-building step.)

Combating Fear with Intuition

"But," you may ask, "what about our legitimate security needs? Are you advocating that we all leave our doors unlocked and our homes open to strangers?" Not at all.

> One day, when in line at the Post Office, I saw a woman ahead of me with a very active, very friendly, very unfearful little five-year-old girl. The girl was playing around the line, talking to all of us who were waiting. She was about to walk up to a man four or five places behind me. She looked at him, stopped, backed up two steps, pointed at him and said, "Mommy, I don't like that man." She then turned and continued to interact with the rest of us.
>
> The man she pointed to looked ordinary. If the little girl had been reacting to differences in outward appearance, she would have rejected me, the only African-American in the line. But she knew intuitively that there was something wrong in the man's energy. (It was not hard to agree with her!) Her mother, admirably, did not try to convince her that she was wrong ("Go talk to the nice man"), nor did she make her afraid of all people ("Don't ever talk to strangers"). By not intervening, she helped her daughter develop and enhance her own intuition, her own internal guidance.

Noted anthropologist Angeles Arrien speaks of people in our society being "intuition injured." Breaker parents, rather than developing and enhancing their children's intuitive abilities, suppress, ignore, and deny them. Consequently, in situations where intuition is needed to assess a person or action, it simply isn't available.

Connecting with The Other

Many of us recognize that violence is only a symptom of a deeper malady. We do not necessarily recognize that nonviolence is also merely a symptom. It is a symptom of a deeper healing and wholeness, of a world going right. So, instead of trying to practice nonviolence (no one practices violence—they are just violent), let us try to practice the connections that make violence both inappropriate and impossible.

When I tell my "politically correct" acquaintances that I have friends who are members of the National Rifle Association or white militias, their reaction is what I would expect if I told a fundamentalist Christian that I fox-trot with the Devil every Wednesday. The first reaction is disbelief, which is followed by outrage and scorn. I have sold out to "the Enemy." Some question my sanity. A few grudgingly credit me with "courage" for dealing with "those people."

The reality is that each of us is The Other for someone. How I treat others is how I want to be treated by others: with dignity, with respect, and with an open mind. Even if I deplore a person's behavior, I try not to forget that he or she is my brother or sister. Or myself.

Ultimately, Menders are not trying to create a world that works for liberals or conservatives, for progressives or regressives. We want the world to work for all. Everyone, on the Right and on the Left, professes to want this. However, their methods, their analyses, and their notions of "all" are drawn from the Breaker story.

Everyone who wants the world to be a better place has a role to play in our transition to the Mender society, even though right now they see themselves as separate from others who ostensibly have the same goal. For example, the tens of millions of people who voted for Ross Perot in his presidential campaigns are aware of certain aspects of The Mess, including the dire effects of an inflated bureaucracy. The African-American men who descended on Washington, D.C., during the "Million Man March" are aware of other aspects, particularly the disintegrating pressures on the black family.

Both of these groups operate on the basis of essentially the same story: "The world works for only a few. However, we can create a world that works for *all who look, act, and think like us.*"

This story is close to the Mender story. There is a clear recognition that something is wrong and an equally clear resolve to do something about it. But one key ingredient is missing: *inclusivity*. With inclusivity, these stories become part of a powerful movement ushering in the Mender era. Without inclusivity, they are nothing more than reformist versions of the Breaker story.

Do the Perot voters or the Million Man Marchers want The Other to "win"? Do they see that their solution *must* include The Other? Or do they believe that The Mess is actually *caused* by The Other, who must therefore be "defeated"? In most cases, those who could unite to make powerful changes in our society are instead locked by their "I am separate" thinking into fighting each other. In this struggle, only Breaker thinking wins.

All the following groups, plus many more, could be strands of a powerful Mender movement. They all work hard in their attempts to make the world a better place. The one thing they may find most difficult to come to grips with is their own "I am separate" Breaker consciousness.

- Environmentalists and others practicing deep ecology values

- Innovative business people
- "Pro-Life" activists
- Capitalists
- Meditators and spiritual seekers
- "Cultural Creatives"
- Women and others practicing Earth-centered, compassionate feminism
- Anarchists
- Community development workers
- Politicians
- Revolutionaries working within various systems
- Right-wing "New Patriots"
- Social justice adherents
- Postcommunists
- "Million Man March" participants
- "Promise Keepers"
- Sustainable development advocates
- Socialists
- "Pro-Choice" activists
- Artists
- Anti-bureaucracy Perot voters
- Compassionate social activists
- Inclusive spiritual leaders
- "Green Party" members
- Libertarians
- Political dissidents
- Multicultural trainers

The Concept of Inclusive Community

The key to changing your relationship to The Other is to expand your notion of Self to include everyone you see.

All of us in this society form one community. The fact that most of us deny it or are ignorant of it doesn't mean the community doesn't exist. It just means the community is highly dysfunctional.

Everyone riding the No. 8 bus is in the same community. The fact that they are all thinking about their various destinations doesn't mean they don't share the same ride down Mulberry St. All the riders have similar expectations, experiences, and values (not stepping on each other's toes, not stealing from each other, not blocking the exits).

Menders recognize that everyone they see or experience, directly or indirectly, is a part of their community—everyone who is

- Driving on the same highway
- Living on the same street, or in the same neighborhood
- Begging for quarters at the subway stop
- Generating trash
- Regularly recycling
- Riding in the same vehicle
- Riding in a polluting vehicle
- Riding a bicycle
- Watching television
- Refusing to watch television
- Smoking crack cocaine
- Smoking Marlboros
- Drinking beer
- Using products made of wood
- Carrying a gun

- Not carrying a gun
- Inhabiting the wealthy neighborhoods
- Inhabiting the poor neighborhoods
- Working in the same office
- Worshiping in the same church

This is the definition of inclusive community. Most of us find it difficult enough to connect with those who are "like us." Inclusive community seems impossible, especially at the societal level. However, just because we have never experienced it does not mean we cannot achieve it.

Some Exercises in Seeing Inclusive Community

- When driving, see the people around you as family and friends, not anonymous enemies trying to take something away from you. Notice whether this changes how you drive.
- Collect the names, addresses, and telephone numbers of all your immediate neighbors. Give them yours. (If you saw smoke coming from a neighbor's house, could you call to warn them?) Talk to them regularly about your neighborhood concerns.
- Go to Safeway or K-Mart. Get in line. The people in front of you and in back of you are part of your community. Start talking to them about their issues.

Steps You Can Take to Include The Other

In order to weave the tapestry of the Mender society from the above threads, you have to

- *Practice diversity.* Really. Not the easy kinds of diversity, like ethnicity and sexual preference. The real test is ideological diversity: can you be tolerant of those who *think* differently? Not tolerant in order to change them, but tolerant despite the differences? Can you practice diversity by recognizing that everyone, including those who oppose your way of living, is important to the tapestry?

- *Practice inclusivity by eliminating artificial boundaries.* If you are organizing a meeting, make sure that anyone who may be talked about is invited to participate.

- *Stop thinking that you are "separate" or "different" (superior or inferior).* Look for common ground with The Other, in action and belief. The linkages are always there.

- *Interact with The Other.* Stop making enemies out of potential allies. When we play the "blame game," we separate from, alienate, and oppose those who are searching, in their own way, for a better society. Remember: you might be wrong about "Them." Your interactions with The Other may be on your terms and your turf, on neutral ground, or on their terms and turf. Choose what is best for all.

- *Get direct with people.* Whenever possible, choose face-to-face contact, not communication by e-mail, Internet, or even telephone. These devices are useful, sometimes even necessary, but they should not substitute for human interaction.

- *Stop letting fear dictate your actions.* Fear keeps the Mender story from coalescing. Stop being defensive. Examine your own heart for the vestiges of bigotry. Few if any bigots think of themselves as such. Most bigots think there are good, noble, and rational reasons for discriminating against "The Other." And each bigot sees wide differences between his own brand of bigotry and others' discrimination.

- *Take the time to tie the threads together.* Each of us is so busy, so focused on our individual thread, so bent on "fixing things" from our own perspective, we miss the larger opportunity: to fundamentally rethink and restructure society.

- *Ultimately, stop seeing The Other.* Recognize when your perception is based on automatic thought processes. The Other is just a way of seeing; you can choose other ways.

PART TWO

A New Analysis for a New Society

Breaking Down, Breaking Through— or Both?

A S DISCUSSED IN Chapter 1, conditions can force us to change and can become the impetus for growth. But how can we tell the difference between negative conditions that are precursors of a positive new reality and those that are precursors of a major catastrophe?

> While having lunch with Michael Dowd, the author of *Earthspirit*, I said something about "the problem." He stopped me immediately. "Sharif, what if there is no problem? What if everything is just in process? A child who can't tie her shoes or another child who can't ride his bike doesn't have a problem—they just haven't grown up yet. Maybe our species just hasn't grown up yet."
>
> There was much deep truth in what Michael said. My response came after a few moments of reflection.
>
> "We are in agreement that the issue for a three-year-old trying to ride a two-wheeler is evolutionary. He will eventually develop both balance and strength to ride the bike.

"A sixteen-year-old on crack cocaine, a thirty-year-old exposed to nuclear radiation, or a society consuming resources faster than they can ever be replaced has different issues. They are not on a path of evolution but on a path of destruction. There is a difference.

"A two-year-old who fails at tying her shoes does not have a problem—evolution will work in her case. A sixteen-year-old who fails at tying his shoes because his brain is fried on drugs has a problem, not a process. The only way his condition will get better is through a quantum leap in a different direction, not more and better drugs."

Breakdown is continued movement in the Breaker direction. *Breakthrough* is a quantum leap in the Mender direction.

There are those who say that breakdown is a necessary phase—that we cannot have breakthrough unless we experience breakdown. But even if they are right, it is evident that breakdown does not *guarantee* subsequent breakthrough. Regardless of crisis and calamity, Breakers have not learned, do not learn, and will not learn. They walk merrily along the road to ruin, crunching the carcasses of dead canaries as they go.

Despite the catastrophic disasters at Chernobyl and Three Mile Island, and the ongoing slow-motion nuclear disaster at the Hanford Nuclear Reserve in Washington State, Breakers still build nuclear power plants. They remind me of people I have visited in the hospital who, fresh from operations for throat cancer, inhale cigarette smoke through the tracheal hole carved in their windpipe. Such patients, like Breakers, have a problem, and no amount of learning or life-threatening conditions can help them see it. The threat of meltdown has no awakening effect in Breaker societies.

In Keeper societies, the threat of meltdown is not needed for the consciousness of sustainability to develop. The Balinese and the Amish live at peace with themselves and their neighbors, and within the regenerative capacity of the Earth. They have not had to flirt with genocide, homicide, and other social disasters in order to achieve their balance.

Menders, in the words of Barbara Marx Hubbard, have to be able to distinguish what is breaking down from what is breaking through.[17] And we must understand that the two processes are occurring simultaneously. It would be a mistake to believe that we are witnessing only one or the other.

In the face of these intertwined phenomena of breakdown and breakthrough, what is our role? According to David Korten, author of *When Corporations Rule the World* and *The Post-Corporate World,*"[18] we have a dual role: hospice and midwife.

For the declining Breaker society, our role is to compassionately assist in its death process, trying to ease the burden and pain of its passing. This includes restraining the impulse for revenge among those who see their foundations undermined by the new. The attitude of defeated Iraqi forces in the Gulf War was "If we lose, you will lose also." They deliberately set fire to the Kuwaiti oil fields, precipitating an ecological and financial disaster of epic proportions. Theirs was a classic Breaker reaction. As the transition to a new society takes place, that reaction must be held in check.

For the emerging Mender society, our role is to compassionately assist in the birth of a new way of acting in the world. As with any birthing process, there will be some pain and trauma associated with the Mender birth. Our role is to minimize the pain and nurse the new society to full health.

The next three chapters will provide us with ways to see what is breaking down and what is breaking through.

4

Stop Blaming Others— You Are the Problem!

Emptying Ourselves of Outmoded Beliefs

TOGETHER, WE ARE writing the script for a new society. To develop this new story, we must be ready to receive new ideas, new insights, new information. The only way we can be open to the new is to empty ourselves of the old, the outmoded, the inappropriate. Zen teachers remind us that just as an already full teacup cannot hold any more tea, a person already full of concepts cannot hold wisdom.

The problem is that some of our limiting thoughts have been with us for so long, they have become our "sacred cows," and as cows do in India, they block the traffic—of ideas. But unlike India's cattle, these thought-cows have no life independent of our consciousness. Slaughtering them will only make the world better for all.

We must root out the fallacies and illusions that create, support, and sustain Breaker society. Before European explorers could cross the ocean, they had to see through the fallacy that the earth was flat and that they would fall off the edge, to be devoured by monsters. We are subject to similar illusions, ones that block our manifestation of a better world. Like the explorers, we have to get over our fear of falling off the edge.

But the question is, What is our "edge"? Where is our illusion?

Taking Off the Blinders

You are changing the tire on a car. You are wearing blinders, so all your attention is focused on changing that one tire. You cannot see that the reason the car doesn't move is not the flat tire but that the engine is missing and the car is on fire. You remain fixated on the flat, focusing all of your attention on the lugnuts. You are oblivious to the fact that by the time you've changed the tire, there won't be any car left to drive.

The car is our society. The blinders are our Breaker conditioning, the thing that keeps us focused in a certain direction. The missing engine is a mission or vision for America. What are we for? What is the definition of "America" that isn't simply a reaction to some perceived threat? The fire is the urgency of our situation: we do not have another two hundred years, or even two hundred months, to figure this out. The lugnuts are the presenting symptoms of our social, political, and environmental crises. Fixing the symptoms cures nothing.

Taking off the blinders means releasing ourselves from some of our most cherished notions and pet theories about how the world works.

Avoiding Responsibility and Denying Power

If you are not motivated to change, you are not paying attention. We no longer have the luxury of acting as though The Mess was someone else's problem or responsibility. No one escapes the effects of the Breaker society.

If you leave the work of change to others, they may either do nothing or simply replicate the problem in another form. But if each of us adopts the attitude "Change begins with me," we will be able to create the consciousness, the compassion, and the actions for fundamental change.

We are all waiting for someone else to act, and thus there is no action. I remember speaking with a homeless man in San Francisco who was looking to the U.S. Congress to solve the problem of homelessness. I told him the men and women in Congress didn't have a clue what to do. And if a Congressman represents a constituency that is overwhelmingly middle-class, if he is paid in excess of $100,000 per year, and has a nice house with a sound roof that keeps out the rain, his sense of urgency about homelessness is likely to be tepid. My homeless friend is the one motivated to find a solution.

Many of us mistakenly believe that we are justified in maintaining the status quo because we benefit from the world of exclusivity:

- Timber barons think they benefit from the destruction of the forests.
- Local consumers think they benefit by buying from megastores.
- Young men carrying guns think they benefit from heightened prestige and a facade of power.
- Local governments think they benefit from increased growth.
- Nuclear power workers think they benefit from nuclear power plants.
- Employees think they benefit by working for large corporations.
- Military contractors think they profit from wars and conflicts.
- Consumers think they benefit by buying sweat-shop goods.
- Toxic clean-up crews think they benefit from spills and disasters.
- Lawyers think they benefit from controversy and disputes.

We each believe we benefit from exclusivity because our blinders keep us from seeing how we are connected to the broader consequences of our own actions. Breaker culture narrows our focus to issues of immediate and short-term survival.

As Breakers, we cannot get "objective" enough to see our situation in its totality. Those "social doctors" among us who are trying to find a cure for our societal diseases cannot be relied on to make an accurate diagnosis, *because they too are diseased.*

A key element of exclusivity is the maintenance of denial. This society encourages us to define our problems in such a way that we exclude ourselves as culprits. The problem always originates with "Them." But we are "Them" to others; no matter who we are, somebody thinks we are the villain. If we define social problems solely in terms of other people's "racism," "male chauvinism," or "homophobia," we exclude all of our own negative, destructive behavior. We then have the smug satisfaction that we are not a major contributor to the problems around us.

The Gas Culture

When Exxon trashed Alaska, they were bringing my gasoline to me. They were bringing you your gasoline. Even if I do not buy from Exxon, I am a major contributor to the mind-set of the automobile culture: "Give me plentiful gas, and give it to me dirt cheap."

Did you visit a gas station in the last month? If you are typical of my seminar participants, 80 to 90 percent of you will answer in the affirmative. If you answer "No," are you the beneficiary of someone else's visit to the gas station? That would be true of anyone who uses a public bus service, takes taxis, or purchases products transported by road. We all contribute.

So we all trashed Alaska. How many of us would be willing to pay the price for ecologically benign, socially responsible fuel?

Assume that a new company springs up in the aftermath of an Exxon Valdez incident: ECO-GAS. It promises to drill, ship, refine, and deliver its product with all possible attention to environmental and social concerns. When the gas hits the market, it costs $4.50 a gallon. How long do you think the company will be in business? How much of *your* money will ECO-GAS get? How many of us are willing to pay a large premium for oil that is shipped in double-hull ships and other safe containers and refined without polluting local environments? Would we accept a $2.00 surcharge on every taxi or bus ride?

The reality is that when Texaco is one penny cheaper than Amoco, I buy from Texaco. We're not talking dollars, we're talking pennies. And every petroleum company executive knows this.

We all answer questions about our priorities every minute of every day. And the staff economists employed by the petroleum companies read those answers as they are translated into market share. The companies ship oil in single-hull tankers because we ask them to. We ask them when we vote with our pennies for the cheapest gas.

I help create and support that system. I own and maintain it. Once that is recognized, the door opens to acting with a higher level of responsibility. I can begin the process of dismantling the system.

Accepting responsibility is empowering. A philosophy that sees us as creators and maintainers of The Mess will also assign us a role in the creation and maintenance of the solutions. One reason why nothing seems to change is that many of us who want to initiate effective change do not realize that we have the power to do so.

Humans Aren't Destroying the Earth— Breakers Are

A key aspect of our denial is our ascription of Breaker behavior to "human nature." Even when we Breakers admit that our actions are destabilizing and self-destructive, we try to blame them on inherent tendencies of the human race: "It is in Man's nature to destroy" or "Humans are innately violent." Those in the environmental movement pick up on this Breaker theme when they talk about "humans" destroying the Earth.

If "humans" are destroying the planet, when did we start? Were we destroying it one million years ago, when humans first controlled and used fire? Or five hundred thousand years ago, when we began building and living in houses? Did Native Americans start destroying North America when they arrived over thirty-five thousand years ago?

No. Humans have been living sustainably and in harmony with the Earth for over a million years, placing no burdens on our planet that it could not bear. In present-day Keeper societies, where Breaker influence is minimal, humans still live in harmony with the Earth.

Let me be quick to add that I am not, in the words of Ken Wilber,[19] a "retro-Romantic." I am not idealizing or romanticizing Keeper societies, any more than I am romanticizing passenger pigeons or buffalo when I point out that the Breaker story also wiped them out. The things Keepers did to maintain their stability are considered cruel by today's standards. Their population control technologies were crude: they limited their populations by killing their children. They rejected outside threats to their local ecology by killing anyone who was a stranger to that ecology.

Nevertheless, Keepers lived sustainably on Earth. They did so because it is a survival strategy that has been hard-wired into every living organism on this planet. Our challenge as Menders is to consciously accept this imperative and to apply it to the entire planet.

Breakers Have Destabilized Our Planet

Wherever it has spread, Breaker consciousness has destabilized indigenous Keeper societies and the ecological balance. However it has spread, whether by military, missionary, mercantile, or other means, it has disrupted an existing harmony. This is a very modern phenomenon. If the history of the Earth is thought of as a movie that is one year long, humans have been a part of the movie for eleven minutes, and Breakers first appeared on the screen only two seconds ago. (See Lester Milbrath's analogy of the yearlong movie in Chapter 5.)

According to one argument, it is the sheer numbers of humans that are destabilizing our ecologies. This, of course, is just another way of describing the Breaker scenario. Breakers do not believe they have to limit their populations the way Keepers and all other beings have done for millions of years. Expansion beyond all limits is not a "human" trait, it is a Breaker trait.

The devastating impact of Breaker consciousness is most clear where Breakers have encountered isolated microecologies: islands. Before the arrival of the Breakers in Hawaii (says a venerable oral tradition), the local Keeper societies had been living sustainably on the islands for twenty-five thousand years or more. Less than one hundred years later, the islands had become unsustainable. This picture repeats itself wherever Breaker consciousness has been introduced. It took a little more than four hundred years for Breakers to destabilize "Turtle Island," the Native American name for North America; the only reason the process took longer than in Hawaii is that Turtle Island is bigger.

There has never been a point when Breaker society was stable. But Breakers have been able to deny this reality and delay the inevitable by constantly exporting their problems elsewhere. Now, there is nowhere else.

The Responsibility Vacuum

We have created a system that is not under anyone's control. Our present problems are too complex to have been created by or controlled by any one person or group.

THE AIRPLANE

We are sitting in a jetliner. It is headed for a mountain. There is no one in the cockpit. We are about to crash. I am yelling at the man sitting in the seat beside me: "DO SOMETHING! Can't you see we're about to crash?!"

While I am doing this, a woman is behind me, hitting me over the head with an umbrella, saying to me: "DO SOME-THING!! Can't you see we're about to crash?!!"

The man beside me says, "Stop screaming at me! I'm not in control!" I say the same thing to the woman behind me. She continues to hit me, screaming, "Well, somebody's got to be in control, and you're sitting in front of me! You got your beverage service first!"

Finally, we all recognize we are strapped in our seats and none of us is able to influence the course of the plane. The woman behind me suddenly shouts: "It's those people in first class! Look at them sipping champagne and munching chocolates while we're about to crash! Let's get them and make them turn this plane around!"

If you are like most of my seminar participants, you probably balk at this analogy. It's a hard one to swallow. Surely *somebody* has to be flying this plane!

There are a few simple tests to determine if anyone is "steering" our society:

- Are *you* responsible for creating The Mess? If you deny this, what makes you think wealthy people, white males, transnational CEOs, military generals, and others who you think are steering are lying when *they* deny creating The Mess?

- Ask the ones who you think are steering if they can change course.

  For example, if you think the President of the United States controls our nuclear stockpile, ask him to dismantle it. If he cannot, he's not in control. (Or ask for something simpler, like universal health coverage.)

Ask the CEO of a transnational corporation if she can stop overproducing, cut back short-term profiteering, employ Americans instead of near-slave labor abroad, invest in environmentally responsible projects—and keep her job.

Just because someone claims to have power does not mean that he does. Having a steering wheel in front of you that does not work, that does not allow you to change course, is just about the same as not having one. A steering wheel you are forbidden to touch is no less useless than one with a lock on it. If the steering wheel is rigged with explosives, so that an attempt to change direction will kill you, making that attempt may be an opportunity for martyrdom, but it is not a realistic option for change. A steering wheel that does not provide you with the power to steer falls under the heading "the trappings of power." While such trappings may be gratifying to your ego, you still are not steering.

The problems of our modern world are not the fault of Democrats or Republicans; communists or capitalists; Europeans or the Third World, none of whom are in control. They are not the fault of the rich or the poor, traditional religionists or New Age chanters, mainstream politicians or Aryan Nation fanatics. Those groups are not in control either. The problems are so complex, they cannot be laid at the doorstep of anyone. No one is to blame, because no one is in control.

THE ICEBERG

We are all cruising along in our luxury liner. Some of us are in first class, with great food, fine wine, the best of everything. Others of us are laboring away in the boiler room, shoveling coal, breathing toxic fumes, cursing our existence. The goal of those in the boiler room is to become first-class passengers.

Our liner strikes an iceberg. It's on its way down. All of us, first-class passengers and boiler-room crew, should be heading for the life rafts, but none of us is budging. The first-class passengers do not believe it is in their best interests to give up their material pleasures for the discomforts and uncertainty of a life raft. The boiler-room folks are still trying to get to first class—they have been struggling for so long, it's difficult to give up their goal and get on the rafts. And if the ship were in danger of sinking, wouldn't the first-class passengers be leaving the ship?

Some of us hold out hope that someone will come along and rescue us, or that the ship will go down so slowly it may take a lifetime to do so. Neither group realizes that the ship is about to explode.

On a sinking ship, salvation does not lie in acquiring more and more resources; it lies in getting off the vessel. However, the average person living a materially abundant life in our sinking Breaker society is not planning an escape—she is trying to figure out how to get more stuff. The man on welfare and in public housing is not thinking about how to create a new society—he is spending all of his money on lottery tickets to gain admission to what he perceives to be first class. Each believes it is not in his or her best interests to abandon the sinking system.

Some of us are trapped in the Breaker system and have abundant resources. Some are trapped with no resources. Regardless of resources, we're all trapped—unless we see beyond the dominant story to a range of greater possibilities.

Auto-Totality:
The Totalitarian State on Autopilot

As Václav Havel says in *The Power of the Powerless,* our world today is marked by Auto-Totality. Auto-Totality is like a totalitarian system, but unlike the monarchist, fascist, or communist systems with which we are familiar, Auto-Totality is not created or kept in place by military force or secret police. It is not maintained by a ruthless ruler or elite, using intimidation, coercion, and carefully calibrated rewards and punishments. It is kept in place by me. It is kept in place by you. It is created by all of us. Collectively, our millions of actions every day create, support, reinforce, and maintain a system where no one is free. Auto-Totality is totalitarianism on autopilot.

In traditional dictatorships, kicking out the ruling clique meant that something changed. Under Auto-Totality, we keep kicking out the incumbents, but the beast lives on. The problem is not bad people but a bad system. Sending good people to Congress does nothing. If I could clone myself 550 times, so that Sharif could occupy every seat in Congress, every seat in the Senate, plus a few extras for the Presidency and the Supreme Court, we would *still* have The Mess. The problem is not the people.

Once we finally get it through our heads that no one is in control of our disastrous predicament, what do we do? *Anything is more useful than beating up on each other.* If we listen, we will hear suggestions coming from all sides. People will be drawing on their intelligence, intuition, collective wisdom, and instinct as they grapple with the oppressive reality. Perhaps one of their proposals will work. Perhaps none of them will. However, exploring these options draws us together and builds a communal strength that generates further creativity and a will to change.

Blaming, Shaming, and Guilt-Making

What if we could in fact find the person or persons who set our society on its present deadly course? What good would it do to assign blame to them? Does assigning blame change anything? Blaming others for The Mess is a luxury we can no longer afford. It steals our energy and our already limited time.

The Toxic Waste Dump

In my seminars, our social ills are compared to toxic waste dumps. Years ago, someone created these poisonous lakes of noxious materials. Does it really matter who? Does it really matter who created the Breaker society? Will assigning blame eliminate either scourge? Or are we going to have to clean it up anyway?

You may say that assigning blame will get those who benefited from the creation of the toxic waste dump to pay for the cleanup. And well they should. However, what if they won't? What if they don't admit to what they have done, or they cannot contribute to the restoration? What if their blinders prevent them from seeing their role? What if they have passed on, leaving the burden of the cleanup to us? Do we wait for more harm to befall us before we act to remedy the situation?

A key element in halting the Blame Game is to see that we are all beneficiaries as well as victims. Who has not benefited from the creation of the toxic waste dump? Who does not have a plastic telephone, or a host of other chemically based products? Who has not eaten chemically produced food or worn synthetics as clothing? Who has not contributed to the toxic envelope of Breaker society? Who has not paid for war, death, and destruction with hard-earned tax dollars? Even though many of us are afraid of it, we all benefit from the toxic waste dump, some more than others. Each of us is a villain in somebody else's toxic story. Finding the "bad guy" is as simple as looking in the mirror.

Clinging to the Thoughts of the Dead

We see the corporate monsters that devour the wealth of communities and nations. We still call this "capitalism," but it is unlike any system ever envisioned by Adam Smith. Confronted by a new economic reality, we refer to it in terms of old labels, because our minds are cluttered with obsolete concepts like capitalism and communism.

We've gone from horse-drawn buggies to the Moon and cyberspace in *one lifetime.* The people who drafted the laws granting corporate charters could never have imagined the megamonsters of global corporatism that now inhabit our land. The writers of the Constitution could never have imagined that the phrase "keep and bear arms" would be the cornerstone of a gun-dominated culture of social violence. The founders of the stock market could never have imagined arbitrage, mutual funds, and programmed trading, with millions of transactions made in nanoseconds, not by humans but by preprogrammed computers.

Our world has changed, but our governing principles, philosophies, and behaviors are based on ideas centuries old—ideas that address a world that no longer exists. While we are poised for the twenty-first century, our thinking, systems of government, economic structures, and values still inhabit the seventeenth, eighteenth, and nineteenth centuries. Thomas Jefferson, Adam Smith, René Descartes, Karl Marx, and all the others we studied so diligently in college *never inhabited our world or anything like it.* Though great in their time, they cannot solve our problems now.

The philosophers of seventeenth-century Europe saw a world ruled by scientific determinism. According to Descartes and others, the universe was like a really big clock. To understand its workings meant taking it apart and looking at the pieces. That same consciousness drives today's Breaker scientists to map and manipulate genes.

> *Most of the theories that guide human affairs today were developed more than a century ago. . . . [The theorists] did not fully anticipate the cumulative effects of following their precepts. They never imagined a world of 10 billion people; they never envisaged that people would poison ecosystems and change the earth's climate; they never dreamt that humans would gain the power to create new life forms or to destroy most life. . . . We cannot escape our planetary predicament by relying on past theories.*
>
> —LESTER MILBRATH[20]

The Astrolabe

The astrolabe was an instrument created back in the Middle Ages in Europe to plot and predict the positions of the planets. It was a very complicated piece of machinery. It had to be.

At that time, the Church-dominated institutions of learning considered Earth the center of the universe, with the Sun and other planets revolving around it. As we now know, you cannot accurately predict the movements of the planets if you consider Earth anything other than a minor planet spinning around the Sun. The flawed theory generated an unnecessarily complicated tool. The theologically driven "science" that spawned the astrolabe prevented the scientists of the day from seeing the true relationships of the celestial bodies.

Theories are important. Theories are well-thought-out stories, operating guidelines for getting us through life. As such, they can be comforting and normative. Even theories we may oppose can provide an illusion of safety, normalcy, being in control. Ranting against them gives us a sense of security: we "know" what the problem is.

The theories of long-dead European men that clutter our minds are blinders, preventing us from seeing the full reality of our present situation. Continuing to think those antique thoughts makes us ill-prepared to think our own twenty-first-century thoughts. The blinders reinforce the Breaker society. The only way we can change that society is to take them off.

Preaching to the Choir

If we want to see widespread change in our society, we must address its center. Preaching to the choir, the people on the fringe who already share our vision, will no longer do. Nor will vacuous exercises in political correctness. We must get our hands dirty, and our hearts exposed, by engaging directly with the Heartland.

Jeffrey, a burly white roadworker, came into the fourth of a series of group sessions and laid a card and pamphlet on my table. Even upside down, I could recognize the material from an Idaho Aryan Nations group. "Sharif," he said, "except for you, these are the only people talking to us about how the world is changing. And you're the only one that makes sense."

Not only do the politically correct not talk to Jeffrey, *they think he is the problem.* By being willing to write him off, by imputing sinister intentions to him, the progressive elite lose Jeffrey and vast numbers of others to the rhetoric of hatred.

The Esalen Empowerment Group

A few years ago, I and about a dozen other activists were convened for a gathering at the Esalen Institute in Big Sur, California, by Joanna Macy, Alan AtKisson, and Robert Gilman, Alan and Robert being the editors of *In Context* magazine. The task of the group, which came to be known as the Esalen Empowerment Group, was to write a manual on citizen empowerment.

Early in the process, our group tackled three questions intended to help frame the context for our work:

1. Who are the citizens we intend to empower?
2. Why do we want them to be empowered? Empowerment for what?
3. How do people actually change? I may feel like writing this book, but will people actually be motivated to change by reading it?

These became ultimate questions for the group. As we addressed them in various subgroups, we came up with two basic principles:

1. Empowerment of the Center

Rather than seeking to empower our own identity group, we wanted to empower everyone, especially those we refer to as "the

Center" or, using the term coined by Richard Nixon, "The Silent Majority." We recognized that no change would take place in our society unless the Center changed.

We did not take a lot of time trying to define or identify the Center, since its broad outlines are clear. We know that nurses, office workers, teachers, grocery clerks, bureaucrats, and road-workers are at the Center; college students are near it but nevertheless outside; radicals and fringe activists (Left and Right) are farthest from the Center.

We also recognized that the Center is not a static phenomenon but an ever-changing conglomeration, with people moving in and out as conditions and views shift. Furthermore, "Center" will mean different things depending on the criteria being applied. For example, a person may be at the Center by virtue of her social views yet on the periphery in terms of ecological action.

The mainstream media do not represent the Center as much as pander to it. They are therefore not a gauge of the Center's true thought and focus. Pandering means operating at the lowest common denominator, at the most superficial levels of titillation. As the newsroom saying goes, "If it bleeds, it leads."

Numerous surveys have shown that Americans believe our current systems are dysfunctional, that our society is going in the wrong direction. Most Americans hold the values of a decent, authentic, compassionate society. For example, a large survey conducted by the Center for the American Dream and the Harwood Group revealed the following:

- Americans believe our priorities are out of whack. People of all backgrounds share certain fundamental concerns about the values they see driving our society. They believe materialism, greed, and selfishness increasingly dominate American life, crowding out a more meaningful set of values centered on family, responsibility, and community. People express a strong desire for a greater sense of balance in their lives—not to repudiate material gain, but to bring it more into proportion with the non-material rewards of life.

- Americans are alarmed about the future. People feel that the material side of the American Dream is spinning out of control, that the effort to keep up with the Joneses is increasingly unhealthy and destructive. People are particularly concerned about the implications of our skewed priorities for children and future generations—they see worse trouble ahead if we fail to change course.

- Americans are ambivalent about what to do. Most people express strong ambivalence about making changes in their own lives and in our society. They want to have financial security and live in material comfort, but their deepest aspirations are non-material ones. People also struggle to reconcile their condemnation of other Americans' choices on consumption with their core belief in the freedom to live as we choose. Thus, while people may want to act on their concerns, they are paralyzed by the tensions and contradictions embedded in their own beliefs. In turn, they shy away from examining too closely not only their own behavior, but that of others.[21]

The problem is clearly not a lack of values. The problem is that we do not know how to create the circumstances in which to practice those values.

2. A World That Works for the Center—And All Others

Most of our current social, environmental, political, and economic change agents, no matter what their ideology, hold to a single belief: "The Center is okay." For decades, the operative theory of activism has been that we would help those who are not okay to move toward the Center, so then they would be okay, too.

Economic advocates want poor people to get jobs, because people with jobs are "okay." Housing advocates want people to live in standard housing, because people who have standard housing are "okay."

The theory was never true, and its falseness has never been clearer than today. The Center is far from okay; it is deeply disturbed, a growing cancer within. And many of us who are in the Center know we are in trouble. Regardless of the lack of labels for our malady, we are aware that something is wrong. Those of us who have achieved the media-touted dream of a career, suburban lifestyle, and consumer abundance know that our lives are hollow. As one of my friends said, "I've been on this train for a long time. I just recently realized that there's no town down those tracks— the train just keeps going."

"THE WHITE MAN IS AN ENDANGERED SPECIES"

I was in the middle of a grueling series of workshops: four-hour sessions twice a day for a month. The workshop participants were roadworkers, the bluest of blue-collar workers, primarily white males who had been ordered to be in my workshops on change and diversity. Despite initial hostility, the sessions were going extremely well.

In the middle of a session, Sam, a thin, twenty-something man with blond curls under his baseball cap, raised his hand and said, "The white man is an endangered species!" I smiled, said something to humor him, and continued on. A few minutes later, Sam put up his hand and said something similar. I again turned him off.

His hand went up a third time. "You're not listening to me!" I took a breath and said: "You're right, I'm not listening. We're going to take a five-minute break and I'm going to center myself so that when we come back, I will be listening."

When we returned, I invited Sam to explain his remarks. "It's not the colored people who are in trouble. It's not the women who are in trouble. All of us are in trouble! How can I be concerned about someone else when it's my butt on the line too? I can't respect some movement that doesn't understand that the whole boat is going down! We can't work for the minorities or for the women—we've got to work for everyone!"

Sam was right. He's in trouble and he knows it. Hearing talk about someone else's problems while his are ignored can only infuriate him. As political satirist Molly Ivins once said, "Bubba's in trouble and the only one who acknowledges his trouble is Rush Limbaugh."[22]

We ignore Sam and Bubba at our peril. What happens when someone who feels endangered is not heard? Those who blew up the Murrah Federal Building in Oklahoma City, taking 168 lives, were of the Heartland, not the periphery. Apparently, the explosion was an expression of their emptiness, their spiritual hunger. The Center is not okay.

We have been asking Sam and Bubba to change for the sake of people they don't know and perhaps don't like. No one wants to be pressured, shamed, and manipulated into changing for someone else's sake. This effort creates its own resistance. The most effective way to promote change is to show a person that it is in his own self-interest. The slogan "Save the Earth!" should be amended to "Save Your Own Butt—And the Earth, Too!"

We can advocate changes on the periphery all we want. We can even narrow the definition of our world so that the periphery looks like the whole world. But until we catalyze a shift in consciousness for all 260 million of us in this country, and all 6 billion of us on this planet, nothing significant will change.

Change at the Center

What catalyzes deep change is an appeal to the heart. Compassion has been the most potent force for positive change. People move when they are reminded of their highest values and ideals, and when they see those values embodied in authentic leaders. The appeal to the heart has been at the center of the social movements led by Mahatma Gandhi, Martin Luther King, Jr., Václav Havel, Desmond Tutu, and Myanmar (Burma) dissident Aung San Suu Kyi, for example.

This appeal may take any of a number of forms. King, Gandhi, and Havel moved people by evoking an ethics that transcends rational thought. All three should have been doomed to failure, since those with vested interests in the status quo had all the tools of temporal power at their command. However, those tools were no match for the power of the heart.

Breaker society, with its underlying assumption, "There is not enough," is based on fear. But if we try to scare people into a Mender Society, we will simply sow the seeds of more separation, brutality, and violence. Fear will simply reconstruct the Breaker society with a new face. Civil disobedience without compassion is just noise. Marching without heart is just motion. Speeches without love are just words.

Rather than teaching the Center what it "should" be concerned about, we must work to know the Center's own concerns. We must find the pathways to its heart. Anything less is perpetuating the arrogance that is the hallmark of exclusivity.

5

THE STORY—HOW THINGS GOT TO BE THIS WAY

It's all a question of story. We are in trouble just now because we are in-between stories. The Old Story—the account of how the world came to be and how we fit into it—sustained us for a long time. It shaped our emotional attitudes, provided us with life purpose, energized action, consecrated suffering, integrated knowledge, and guided education. We awoke in the morning and knew where we were. We could answer the questions of our children. But now it is no longer functioning properly, and we have not yet learned the New Story.

—THOMAS BERRY[23]

CHANGING OUR STORY is the fastest and most effective way to change our world. With a changed story, we can move rapidly to change our toxic relationships with the Earth and each other. Once the story changes, the old paradigm becomes unthinkable.

Introduction to The Story

In order to understand how things got to be the way they are in the human world, let's look at how things got to be the way they were on Rabbit Island.

On Christmas Day, 1776, British explorer Captain Cook arrived on Kerguelen Island, a Connecticut-sized land mass covered with grass in the Indian Ocean.[24] One of the things Cook did while he was there was release a few rabbits. He thought the rabbits would provide fresh meat for any sailors who followed.

The rabbits, in a favorable climate with no natural predators, multiplied. And grew. And flourished. And overpopulated. In a short span of time, the rabbit population exploded into the hundreds of thousands, perhaps millions.

Then, after eating every single blade of grass, they died. They died as they lived, by the hundreds of thousands. The old ones died, the baby bunnies died, the pregnant mothers died. They died because that's how the Web of Life works. Biologists call it "overshoot and dieback." No rabbit was immune.

If you go to the island today, you will see that not one rabbit or one blade of grass exists. Both rabbits and grass were rendered extinct by the rabbits' success. The rabbits were killed by their own story.

Each rabbit had a story that governed its existence and behavior: "Creating a World That Works for Me." According to this story, each rabbit maximized its position, eating as much as it could and producing as many offspring as possible. This formula for "success," in the absence of competing owl and coyote success formulas, was fatal. The rabbits were disastrously successful. Exclusivity is death.

Think about how the rabbits must have felt when their population reached a million and "only" half of their grass was gone. They were in Rabbit Heaven! All the grass you could eat (with no competition), half a million sex partners, and not a coyote in sight! Eat, sleep, and screw all day! The only thing they didn't know was that they were just one generation away from annihilation.

Assume that, at this time, a more-reflective-than-average bunny wrote a book entitled *Creating an Island That Works for All*. In it, he said that if they were to continue to thrive, rabbits everywhere on the island would have to change their *thinking*. No more "maximum food, maximum sex." This strange bunny even went so far as to say that rabbits needed eagles, owls, and coyotes! Without them, the rabbit population would outstrip the generative capacity of the island and all would die. In order for the island to work for rabbits, it had to work for coyotes also. The bunny writer called his concept "inclusivity." He believed that if the rabbits consciously reduced their food intake, consciously restricted their sex habits, and invited in a few owls, eagles, and coyotes, the rabbits and the grass would continue to flourish.

We'll never know whether or not the book bunny was right. We do know, however, that the others were wrong. Dead wrong.

The human population has doubled in my lifetime, and given the current rate of growth, is predicted to double again before I die. We are multiplying like rabbits who have no predators. On a planet with finite resources, our exponential growth makes "overshoot and dieback" our likely destiny. Life can do very well without humans on Earth—or rabbits on a particular island.

Think about this the next time you hear about the stock market's continual rise, the Breaker economy's constant expansion, or the human population's inexorable increase. The Breaker story is as much a recipe for disaster for our planet as the Rabbit story was for Kerguelen Island. Our question is simple: Can we change our paradigm, or will we consume all the grass on this particular island called Earth and die off? Can we change stories in time?

We have failed to take into account the long-run consequences of just doing what we have always done—but better and better.

—LESTER MILBRATH[25]

What Is a Story?

According to the book *Ishmael,* we enact a story every morning when we get up. As we get out of bed and brush our teeth, we start living our lives according to a story. This enactment continues in our thoughts, words, and deeds throughout the day.

But what *is* a story? According to *Ishmael,* a story is a piece of our culture that explains

- How we got here
- Where we are going
- The interrelationships between ourselves, our environment, and the invisible forces (spirits, ancestors, guides, etc.)[26]

At an early age, we each were given a story to enact. No one sat us down and said, "Mary, I'm now going to tell you the Story of Our Culture." No one gave us a book emblazoned with that title in gold lettering. What happened was that we looked around and saw everyone doing something. They called it

going to work, catching the bus, catching an antelope, reading a book, reading a palm, conducting a ceremony, conducting a train, eating breakfast, drinking blood, drinking a beer, carrying a gun, tossing rattlesnakes, tossing a salad, killing villagers, making a killing in the market, watching television, watching a sunset, massaging the feet of an elder, visiting the nursing home, making a basket, selling sex, selling stocks and bonds, selling rhino horns, selling military weaponry, stealing a wife, stealing home, stealing a kiss, beating a child, beating a carpet, beating the visiting team, beating a horse, consulting the fortune-teller, consulting a lawyer, consulting the ancestors, consulting the Dow Jones averages, putting on lipstick, putting on cow dung, abstaining from sex, indulging in sex, taking violin lessons, taking drugs, taking a break, driving a car, driving cattle, avoiding the death squads, avoiding taxes, putting on track shoes, putting on high heels, cutting fresh broccoli for a salad, cutting down the rainforest . . .

We saw these things (or, at least, the ones appropriate to our story) and, without question, we began to imitate those around us. If we saw people eating food they had grown, we did the same. If we saw people eating food purchased from the supermarket, we did the same. If we saw people eating grasshoppers and grubs, we did the same.

A parent doesn't really "teach" his or her child to walk. What the parent does is walk in the presence of the child, modeling the behavior. The child imitates this behavior without regard to whether it is an "improvement" on what it was doing before. What would the child know about improvement? At that stage of its life, conformity to the adult norm is good.

No one tells us, as children, to do this modeling. Enacting the story we see is hard-wired into our systems. According to the research of Jean Piaget and other child psychologists, children don't develop the faculty of abstract reasoning until they are around seven years of age. By that time, most children are fully functioning members of their society. This means you were fully practicing your story well before you developed the capacity to understand it. The story is the only reality you know. You don't question it, you do it. And you are taught to treat every other story as a totally ungrounded fantasy. Excluding other stories is integral to the process.

I am sitting in the canteen at Sarvodaya headquarters in Sri Lanka, about to eat my first Sri Lankan meal. On either side of me are Westerners; a young guy from England on one side, an even younger American on the other. We're sitting in front of delicious-smelling vegetarian food. There's only one problem: no forks and knives, no chopsticks, nothing.

All around us, everyone else has literally dived in, handfuls of food disappearing from their plates. The other American and I are still staring at our plates, trying to muster the courage to stick our hands into our food. This is not "finger food" like sandwiches or french fries, this is wet, hot, sticky rice and curry dishes.

Leaning over to the American, I whisper, "Are your Mommy tapes running?" He thinks for a second, then bursts into laughter. "Mom is screaming at me right now! 'Get your hands out of your food! Are you some kind of heathen?!' I'm trying to get her to shut up so I can eat!"

"Mommy tapes" are part of our story. They instruct and admonish us, whatever we are doing.

People *always* enact the story given them by their culture, whether the enactment causes benefit or harm to themselves and others. If the story is beneficial and sustainable, people will enact it. If the story is or becomes dysfunctional, they will still enact it, at their peril and the peril of others. People will enact *any* story, including a dysfunctional one, until given a better alternative.

Just as we can't see our own eyes without a mirror, it is difficult to see our own story unless we compare it with stories from outside our culture. However, there is a problem here: our own story tells us to ignore or reject all of the stories of others. We have names for other cultures' stories: tall tales, mythology, fantasy, cultism, old wives' tales, perversion, barbarism. Our own story, of course, is not a story at all—it's "the Truth."

Culture and Story

Conventional wisdom is the dominant consciousness of any culture. It is a culture's most taken-for-granted understandings about the way things are . . . and about the way to live. . . . It is a culture's social construction of reality and the internalization of that construction within the psyche of the individual. It is thus enculturated consciousness—that is, consciousness shaped and structured by culture and tradition.

—MARCUS BORG[27]

What's the difference between "culture" and "story"? Culture is what happens. Story is the *explanation* for what happens. It explains what we do, how we got here, what our relationship is to all others, and, most important, where we're going. A story provides the reasons for our actions:

- "We plant our crops this way because our ancestors . . ."
- "We pray this way because God spoke to us many years ago . . ."
- "I have to sell drugs because the white man . . ."
- "I beat up that kid who pushed me because being weak is bad . . ."
- "We have to build more nuclear weapons because a strong national defense . . ."
- "Don't trust those people, because last time we trusted them . . ."
- "We are selling cigarettes to Africa because making money makes America strong . . ."
- "Our people are oppressed because an international conspiracy . . ."

Such explanations don't have to be logical, good, or true. Provided the behavior they are explaining appears to work, they tend to be accepted without rational analysis. Consider how three groups of cultures explain their eating habits:

Culture	Custom	Rationale
Western	Eating with a fork	"It's cleaner, it's easier. Hands are dirty. Chopsticks are hard to use. Food tastes better."
Asian	Eating with chopsticks	"It's cleaner, it's easier. Hands are dirty. Forks are hard to use. Food tastes better."
Middle Eastern	Eating with the hand	"Its cleaner, it's easier. Forks and chopsticks are dirty—they've been in someone else's mouth. Food tastes better."

These three eating stories are clearly in conflict with each other, the adherents of each believing they are "right" and the others "wrong," if not dirty and disgusting. But as long as everyone is getting fed, there is no compelling need to challenge the stories.

The Tenacity of Story

Once a person has attached himself to a story, asking him to let go of it makes about as much sense as asking him to die. (Actually, the latter may be easier: people are willing to die by the millions to preserve their story.)

> A radio correspondent interviewed a man who was fighting in the former Yugoslavia. The man said: "I will kill and I will gladly be killed to maintain my identity as a Kosovo Albanian. Being a Kosovo Albanian is more important than life itself!"
>
> The majority of Americans listening to the broadcast were probably wondering what exactly a Kosovo Albanian was.

In our Keeper past, the survival of the narrow group was synonymous with the survival of the individual. Today, it is the survival of the entire planet on which each of us depends. The story we are now defending, the Breaker Story, is a collective myth of destruction.

We need a new story.

Stories That Fit

A Navajo child is given a story to enact. A Manhattan child is given a very different story to enact. Which story is "right"? In reality, neither is right or wrong. The real question is, Which story is appropriate to the world in which those children will in all likelihood live? The Navajo child is given a story that helps her navigate a desert; a Hawaiian child is given a story that helps him navigate an island and the sea; the Manhattan child is given a story that helps her navigate one specific type of urban environment.

A friend who teaches elementary school in Alaska's Arctic Circle regions related a story to me. "I was giving a geography lesson, pointing out various places on the globe. I asked the children how they would travel from New York to London. Their answer was immediate: 'Dog sled!' I told them that the Atlantic Ocean was not frozen. Again, their answer was immediate: 'Wait for it to freeze, then go by dog sled!' I told them the Atlantic Ocean never freezes solid. There was stunned silence in the room. One boy raised his hand and said, *'Everything* freezes.'

"I'm not sure I was doing them a favor. In their world, everything does freeze solid. That is a much more important reality to them than what I was teaching."

Each child's upbringing is inappropriate for the others. They each would be ill-equipped for survival in the others' environments. The bunnies on Rabbit Island had a story that was appropriate to a world that contained predators, but completely, fatally inappropriate to a world without predators.

In workshops with contractors, many of them tell stories about the difficulties they faced building government housing for Native Americans on reservations. In the early days, the houses would collapse or go up in smoke in the first few days of occupancy. The Indians were not malicious; they weren't vandals. The houses collapsed from a clash of stories.

The Native American story for "house" is "a place where everyone gathers in the same room" or "a place to build a fire." To accommodate their story, they would remove all of the interior walls (causing the house to collapse) or build a fire in the center of the living room (causing the house to burn down).

The Breaker style of housing, based on exclusivity, was wholly incompatible with the Native American story.

There is nothing wrong with the Breaker Story as a story. The problem is that it is the dominant story, trying hard to be the only story. "I am separate," by itself, is not a problem. Thinking objectively is not a problem. The problem arises when "I am separate" becomes the *only* story, because there are vital elements missing from it. Like the rabbits on Rabbit Island, Breakers are not "wrong," they are disastrously inappropriate.

Seven Elements of a Successful Story

What are the elements of a successful story? That depends, of course, on your criteria for success.

The Nazi story, "Creating a World That Works for Aryans," was successful if the criteria for success include the elimination of a significant portion of the population. The industrial story, "We Can Grow Forever," was successful if the criteria include exhaustion of the planet's resources. The slavery story, "Creating a World That Works for Whites," was successful if the criteria for success include exploitation and oppression of other human beings. The scientific determinism story, "We Know Everything," is successful if the criteria for success include suppression of the world of the spirit.

But since these are not our criteria, success must be identified in other ways. Here are seven important elements (you may add others):

To be successful, a new story must be

1. *Inclusive.* The story must have a positive role for every individual and every group. Any story that shames, blames, or ridicules any group is doomed to failure. So are stories that involve mass incarceration or genocide.

2. *Authentic.* Values and actions must be in harmony.

3. *Spiritual.* The story must articulate and demonstrate transcendent values and beliefs. It must include roles for the spirits,

ancestors, and other invisible beings, depending on religion or belief system.

4. *Scapegoat-free.* No person or group is made a repository of blame or condemnation.

5. *Sustainable.* The story must pass the test of the seventh generation: will it produce benefits, and cause no harm, to seven generations in the future?

6. *Positive, creative, and adaptive.* The story has to be able to evolve with emerging conditions and events.

7. *Practical, implementable.* The story can be enacted now, without extraordinary innovations (such as contact with space aliens) or materials (such as cheap, safe, inexhaustible fuel).

In the Nazi story, an obvious failure, almost all of these elements were absent. National Socialism was

1. Elitist rather than inclusive.
2. Based on consensual lies rather than authenticity.
3. A travesty of spirituality.
4. Dependent on the existence of a scapegoat.
5. Unsustainable because it was based on the constant expansion of military and political power.
6. Positive, creative, and adaptive—for the elite only.
7. Tragically practical in the short run.

Living Between the Stories

As an entire society, we are between stories. We know the story of the eighteenth, nineteenth, and early twentieth centuries: "Manifest Destiny"—"We must explore and conquer the land, because it is our God-given duty as Americans to extend our borders." We know the story of the mid- to late twentieth century: "Fighting Communism"—"We must pour billions of dollars into armaments and the support of numerous regimes around the world because we have to resist the spread of Communism."

What's our story now? We briefly flirted with the space race as the vertical extension of both the Manifest Destiny and Fighting Communism stories. However, except for a few rocket jockeys, we can't enact a space race story.

Many different stories are now vying to capture the hearts and minds of Americans. They include

Consumption/Success Stories
"Shop Till You Drop"
"Lifestyles of the Rich and Famous"
"Upward Mobility"
"Martha Stewart Living"
"Stocks to Watch"
"Small Is Beautiful" (anticonsumption)

Exploitation/Persecution Stories
All colonization stories
Religious persecution (Judaism, Mormonism)
Ethnic persecution
Feminism
Gay/lesbian/transgender rights
Disability rights
Animal rights

Liberation Stories
World War II
Vietnam War
Gulf War and anti-Saddam struggle
Save the Earth

Revolution/Salvation Stories
People-led revolutions
Spiritual revolutions
Cults
UFOs

Discovery Story
   "The Frontiers of Science"

Distraction Stories
   Alcohol
   Drugs
   Gambling
   Sex
   Entertainment
   Electronic media
   Sports

Image Stories
   Cosmetic surgery
   "No pain, no gain": the gym as second home
   "Dress for Success"
   Anorexia/bulimia
   Piercing/tattooing/scarification

The Three Stories of History

There are three major stories that have shaped or are shaping the behavior of humans on this planet:

The Original Story: "The Keepers"

The Dominant Story: "The Breakers"

The Emerging Story: "The Menders"

Essence of the Stories

We Are Keepers . . . We live our lives in harmony with "all our relations." We act out of the belief that the world was not created for any one species. We live here; we don't try to control life. We keep to the ways that work.

We Keepers have been devastated by the Breakers. For thousands of years, the Breakers have killed us, dishonored our ancestors, destroyed our food, ruined our magic, forced us to their ways. The Breakers have been at war with the Earth, and we have suffered for it. The Breakers call us by many names, most of them bad: primitives, savages, natives, aborigines, heathens, pagans, the uncivilized.

Despite this history, we hope that our brothers and sisters who are Breakers will change their ways and come into balance with the Earth, with each other, and with us.

We Are Breakers . . . The Earth and everything in it were created for Man; we have the right and the responsibility to place all of it under our control. Because there is not enough for all, the world must be conquered in order for us to exist. We do not live in the Web of Life; we live on top of it. Our story is simple: wildness is bad, human control is good.

We call ourselves by many names, most of them positive or benign: civilizers, settlers, pioneers, missionaries, explorers, industrialists. We will continue to control and dominate all life forms, including humans who are not like us, because control is good.

We Are Menders . . . We believe the Earth and our fellow humans need to be healed from the excesses of exclusivity, and we live our daily lives in accordance with this belief. We used to be Breakers, but are consciously turning away from that dead-end path, away from the glitter and allure of the Breaker society. Our goal is to live as a consciously integral part of a living, conscious, and sacred planet, to catalyze a new era, the Mender era.

Our task is simple and profound: to heal the damage caused by the Breakers, those who act as though the Earth and all of her inhabitants were their property. We vow to stop Breaker destruction and begin to restore the balance between the Earth and humanity within this generation.

We Menders are Breakers in recovery. Breaker history is our history. We are not arrogant enough to think that our problems are someone else's fault. We consciously reject all privileges that have come to us at the expense of others' lives, freedom, or comfort.

The Mender story is in harmony with an ancient story, one as old as the Earth itself. We honor the Keepers, who show us the way of wisdom. We honor the Breakers, who show us the way of technology. We heal the damage. We are Menders.

A Synopsis of the Stories

The **Keeper story** is the original story of humans. Keepers are people who live interconnected with their local ecologies and all other beings. They keep the ancient ways of living, perfected over eons of coexistence. Their story is based on a thought, "Living in harmony with all I encounter," and an assumption, "The land is abundant."

Keepers do not have a concept of the Earth as a whole; they are identified with their local ecologies. Within those ecologies, they have, over the course of a million years or more, achieved a dynamic equilibrium with all beings, including human and non-material beings.

Together with their environment, Keepers form a *holobeing*. As a functioning whole, this holobeing repels all invaders.

When Keepers travel to a new ecology, after some period of adjustment, they again arrive at a dynamic equilibrium with the environment.

The ultimate expression of the Keeper story is the village, constructed with local materials and interrelated with the local ecology.

The **Breaker story** is at present the dominant story for humans. Breakers are those of us who act as though everything on and in the Earth were created for us, and that we have the right and responsibility to place it all under our control. The Breaker story is based on a thought, "I am separate," and an assumption, "There is not enough." Breaker behavior is based on control and manipulation of other beings.

Breakers force food to grow in surplus, believing they do not have to be concerned with the ecological consequences of their actions. They force rice to grow in the desert, killing off the beings who live in the desert ecosystems. They prevent other beings from eating the food Breakers grow, destroying beneficial plants, animals, and insects and disrupting forever the local ecological balance. By extending their control over ever greater areas of their environment, Breakers move further out of touch with Nature.

When Breakers travel to another ecology, they completely alter or destroy that ecology in an effort to make it optimal for themselves. All other beings, including other human beings, are either domesticated or eliminated.

The ultimate expression of exclusivity is the city, where Nature is almost totally suppressed. It is worth noting that "civilized" values are those associated with city (Latin, *civitas*) life.

The **Mender story** is the emerging story for humans. Menders are people who are conscious of the global ecology and the interactions of all of the beings who make up that ecology. Menders adapt the values of Keepers to a global reality. The Mender story is based on a thought, "We are One," and an assumption, "There is enough for all."

Menders recognize that humans have become the world's first global species. From the North Pole to Antarctica, there is no local ecology that does not contain humans. Keepers have an ethic that keeps them in harmony with one local ecology. Menders are creating a story that will bring global human behavior back in line with the regenerative capacity of the Web of Life.

Menders dedicate their lives to restoring the balance, integrity, and regenerative capacity of the Web of Life.

Details of the Stories

*What does it mean to live outside ecosystems? It means that our
interests no longer dovetail with those of the natural world around
us. . . . Inventing agriculture in a very real sense was tantamount
to declaring war on local ecosystems.*

—NILES ELDREDGE[28]

A few thousand years ago, Breakers started us all on a spiral of destruction. In the twinkling of an epochal eye, the Breaker practice
of exclusivity has threatened to render the planet virtually unin-
habitable and human relations a suicidal, homicidal, demoralized,
disenchanted, radioactive tragedy.

Lester Milbrath speaks eloquently about the nature of this
change in his book, *Envisioning a Sustainable Society.* He compares
the history of our planet to a yearlong movie. If the movie starts
in January and ends (at the present) in December, life itself shows
up in March. He goes on to state:

*Compared to most other species, humans have lived on planet
earth for a very brief time, (only 11 minutes of our year-long
movie). During most of that time humans have lived in harmony
with nature; their home was that environment in which they
evolved. It is only very recently that our species created an unnatural home for itself as it set out to dominate nature. In that brief
period (only two seconds of our year-long movie), we have built a
civilization that cannot sustain itself.[29]*

In the short space of ten thousand years (two seconds of Milbrath's movie), Breakers have destroyed, disrupted, and stressed every
living system on this planet. (They call this "progress.") Breakers
have developed the capacity to end all human life, and most other
life as we know it on Earth—no small feat, given the fact that when
they started, the most powerful human artifice was a spear.

Even after the drastic reductions in nuclear weapons brought about by treaties, the world's nuclear powers presently have enough destructive capacity to kill thirty-two billion people. There are fewer than six billion on the planet right now. The equivalent of 1.7 tons of TNT exists for every man, woman, and child now living on Earth.[30] This does not take into account our biological and chemical weapons of mass destruction.

We don't have to wait for the Breakers to finally destroy the world to know that they eventually will. We can no longer afford to maintain the fiction that Breaker consciousness is viable. Enough of us know that the ship is going down. Some of us are actively looking for the exits. Some of us are working to change our collective consciousness, our behaviors, and our institutions.

It Ain't All Bad

The Breaker record is not entirely negative, however. In fact, it includes some of humanity's finest achievements.

These words are being written in Havana, Cuba, on the seventh floor of a Fifties-era condominium that faces the glittering blue waters of The Malecon. When I'm done, my laptop computer will be put away and I will eat a delicious lunch. Later this evening, I will take a taxi to a salsa club and listen to some great music. None of this would be possible without the Breaker story.

Without the separating consciousness of Breakers, few of the materially beneficial parts of my life would exist. This consciousness has yielded wonderful results in the fields of health, science, world exploration, commerce, and entertainment. Up until one hundred years ago, the majority of humans lived their entire lives within fifty miles of their birthplace; now, going around the world is not uncommon. Breakers have been able to wipe out polio and smallpox, while controlling malaria and many other diseases that debilitated humans by the millions. They have done this at a very small environmental cost.

The problem is that, like the rabbits on Rabbit Island, Breakers do not know how and when to stop. They splice human genes onto tomato plants to make the tomatoes redder. They have the technology (intelligence about things) to do this, but lack the wisdom (intelligence about relationships) to know *not* to do it.

Parts of Breaker and Keeper thought are essential to the long-range purpose of Earth. Breaker thought allows us to see the world *objectively,* a capacity that can enhance life. Keeper thought allows us to see the world *relationally,* which helps us build our connections with each other. Menders are the blend of these two forms of thought.

Breaker consciousness, which liberated people from local ecologies and brought about an explosion of self-awareness, represented an evolutionary step for humanity; Menders represent the next evolutionary step: bringing human behavior in line with the needs of the Earth.

We are facilitating a fundamental shift from the destructive aspects of Breaker thought. The Breaker mind-set is only a powerful consciousness, a thought. That consciousness can be changed with a different thought.

Menders understand that someone has to repair the damage caused by Breakers, aspects of which will last hundreds of thousands of years. For example, Menders will need to care for the Breakers' nuclear waste dumps. Some of that waste will remain deadly for more than one hundred thousand years. There are 257 tons of plutonium in the world. Only 330 pounds are necessary to kill every human on the planet.[31]

We recognize that living in this world is a sacred act. We behave in ways that heal and restore balance—in our lives, in our communities, in the world. Menders live with wisdom. Menders practice inclusivity. Menders think holistically.

The astronauts gave us our first practical vision of holistic thinking. Although we have known that we live on a round ball since before 1492, it was the space program that gave us the picture of what we really look like as a planet. The Apollo astronauts and Soviet cosmonauts beheld a planet with no lines, no divisions, no right and wrong, no "us" and "other."

This was a startling, paradigm-shifting moment for the astronauts and for those of us on the ground. Until the first images came back to us from space, every globe or map of our planet was seen through Breaker eyes, with borders, political colorings, Cartesian coordinates, and other visual dividers. It was as though the only frogs we had seen were those cut up on the dissection table. The astronauts were the first to see a *living planet*.

The astronauts and cosmonauts gave us a powerful image of what it means to be *homo sapiens holonus,* the thinking human who is part of the whole. In their own words:[32]

> *When I was the last man to walk on the moon in December, 1972, I stood in the blue darkness and looked in awe at Earth from the lunar surface. What I saw was almost too beautiful to grasp. There was too much logic, too much purpose—it was just too beautiful to have happened by accident. It doesn't matter how you choose to worship God . . . God has to exist to have created what I was privileged to see.*
>
> —GENE CERNAN

> *[O]nly when I saw [Earth] from space, in all its ineffable beauty and fragility, did I realize that humankind's most urgent task is to cherish and preserve it for future generations.*
>
> —SIGMUND JAHN

> *With all the arguments, pro and con, for going to the moon, no one suggested that we should do it to look at Earth. But that may in fact have been the most important reason of all.*
>
> —JOSEPH P. ALLEN

*It isn't important in which sea or lake you observe a slick of pol-
lution, or in the forests of which country a fire breaks out, or on
which continent a hurricane arises. You are standing guard over the
whole of our Earth.*

—YURI ARTYUKHIN

The first man in space, Yuri Gagarin, made this atheistic statement on his return: "When I was in space, I looked and looked for
a God, but did not find him." Perhaps he was looking in the wrong
direction.

Menders Are Not Keepers

While we can learn much from the values and wisdom of the
Keepers and the way Keepers are interrelated with each other and
their local ecosystem, it is safe to say that few of us would trade
lifestyles with most Keepers. Just one of many possible stories:

> I was talking with a woman in Uganda, who informed me
> that she had borne a total of nine children, to watch all but
> two die within the first five years of life. In her group, they
> don't even name their children until they are over a year old.
> Her children died from diseases Breaker science has already
> cured: diarrhea, stomach worms, and various viruses.

While learning much from this Ugandan mother, I would not
trade places with her.

The Keeper story is not adaptable enough to survive the
Breakers. Keepers are one with their local ecologies but are not
conscious of their oneness; they simply *are*. The lack of consciousness beyond their local ecosystem is their blind spot, which puts
them at the mercy of those who have a broader view.

The pioneers of the new society, the Menders, are *conscious* of
the global nature of their oneness. Menders seek out opportunities

to practice interconnection and interdependence with other beings. At the same time, we are aware of situations where it is advantageous to think and act in an objective fashion. We could be thought of as *tempered* Breakers, or Breakers with a goal of wholeness, healing, and connection.

Keeper, Breaker, and Mender Consciousness Within Each of Us

You can go to the interior of the Amazon basin and visit Keeper communities. You can go to the interior of the jungles of Manhattan Island and visit Breaker communities: tribes of stockbrokers in lower Manhattan, tribes of public housing tenants in upper Manhattan, all living their lives in accordance with the Breaker "I am separate" thought. (It may not be possible to visit Mender communities yet.)

However, without traveling anywhere, you can visit these three states of consciousness within your own heart.

You have a Keeper self that you can honor:

- Your Keeper self needs wildness and reverence for both ecologic and nonmaterial realities.
- Your Keeper self seeks deep harmony with other beings, including other humans.
- Your Keeper self needs to acknowledge that others (beings, ancestors, spirits) are powerful and to trust their power.
- Your Keeper self has no need to manipulate self or others; it experiences satisfaction in community.

You also have a Breaker self that can be honored (but not allowed to dominate):

- Your Breaker self seeks to be defined and honored as an individual.
- Your Breaker self is restless and hungry; it is the source of your urge to explore and grow beyond your boundaries.

- Your Breaker self needs to be in control—of self, others, and the environment.
- Your Breaker self enjoys manipulating its world.

You can acknowledge your Mender self that is now emerging more clearly in your view:

- Your Mender self seeks to transcend the individual self, and desires transcendent experiences.
- Your Mender self is holistic and ecologic, desires peace and sustainability, and thinks in terms of global realities.
- Your Mender self desires to practice compassion—for self, others, and the more-than-human environment.
- Your Mender self celebrates and explores its differences from and similarities to The Other.

As Menders, we acknowledge, then control, minimize, or eliminate Breaker thinking within ourselves. We recognize that we are carriers of the Breaker Disease. We are committed to not continuing the spread of this consciousness and to purposefully catalyzing Mender thinking, in ourselves and others.

The way we control the excesses of Breaker consciousness is to adopt the values of the Keepers and apply them to the Breaker world. The key Keeper values include wisdom, sacredness, and inclusivity with all beings.

Keepers, Breakers, and Menders: Comparisons

	Keeper Consciousness	Breaker Consciousness	Mender Consciousness
Focus	Life. Keepers see their local environment, including all other beings, as sacred. All beings are part of the Web of Life.	Things. Breakers see their local and distant environments, including all other beings, as property. They treat their environment as a collection of commodities.	Life (primarily). Menders see the total environment, local and global, as sacred, and as "property," to the extent that it benefits the whole.
Highest Priority	Local ecology. No being is more important than another; each has its own unique medicine.	Self. Breakers see "I" as more important than "others."	Global Web of Life.
Characteristic Attitudes	Reverence, honor, and humility before the Web of Life.	Arrogance, dominance.	Compassion.
Relationship to the World	Take what you need with reverence. Ask permission to take it. Use all that you take; leave the rest for others (or later).	Either domesticate or exterminate, control or kill. Take everything, whether needed or not. What is not used is "waste."	Bring life into balance. There is no "waste," only wrong thinking about valuable resources.
Source of Safety	Keepers trust the abundance of the Web of Life.	Safety lies in control.	Safety lies in restoring balance and trust in the Web of Life.
Sustainability	Keepers are sustainable. They have been perfecting their story for one million years or more.	Breakers live on top of the Earth's systems and therefore have no need or desire to be sustainable.	Menders are creating a new story of the sustainability and health of the Web of Life.

6

HOW THE BREAKER STORY
MAINTAINS ITSELF

IF IT IS SO EASY to write a new story, why hasn't someone done this before? Why has the Breaker story been in the driver's seat for over one hundred centuries? What keeps this consciousness in place?

A story represents a group's long-term survival strategy. If a particular story helps the next generation to make it in the world, the story is repeated, refined, and enhanced.

Because we have survived as humans for over one million years and can trace our lineage back to the dawn of life on this planet, the preservation of our survival strategies, including our story, is embedded within our system.

The strong survival story of one species may, unfortunately, be a mixed blessing to others when the favored species is introduced into a new ecological system. The following are just a few examples:

- Kudzu, the vine that is literally devouring the southeastern United States, is a plant with a very strong survival story and no predators or other countervailing forces.
- Brown tree snakes in the South Pacific islands are endangering bird and animal populations.
- Zebra mussels stowed away in the ballast tanks of ships have all but destroyed the marine ecologies in the rivers,

bays, lakes, and other waters the ships visit. Virtually all navigable lakes and rivers have been affected.

- Water hyacinth, a beautiful flowering plant, is killing Lake Victoria in East Africa and threatens the lives of the humans and animals that depend on the lake for their food and livelihood.

In the Pacific Northwest, the logger story, "Cut down as many trees as you can," may have been appropriate when it took twenty men and teams of mules more than a week to cut down and transport one tree. With a technology that allows one person to cut and move twenty trees in an hour, the logger story has led to the decimation of the old-growth-forest ecosystems.

Stories maintain themselves with great tenacity, even when underlying conditions change. Therefore, in order to modify or replace the Breaker story, we need to understand how it keeps itself alive. We will examine four key ways in which exclusivity is maintained:

- Language
- Culture
- Psychological coherence
- Fallacies of power and powerlessness

The Role of Language

Someone wrote that the Hawaiians have over thirty words that describe various conditions of rain. Anyone living in Oregon, under the near-perpetual cloud cover of the Willamette Valley, can really appreciate that fact. Without thinking hard, I can identify over a dozen different types of rain, among them the soft, white rain; the blowing rain; the kind where you don't really get wet enough to put up an umbrella; the rain during sunshine; the cold, foggy rain; the drenching rain . . .

But unlike the Hawaiians, I *don't* have thirty words to describe rain; I have just a few. That does not mean that I do not experience thirty different kinds, it just means I cannot communicate the experience to you.

Many of us feel this same frustration whenever we try to describe our present social condition. There is a huge movement building in this country, and we are ripe for transformation. However, the movement will not mature so long as we lack the ability to transmit our experience of our society to others.

Language is a code of expressions and behaviors that convey commonly agreed upon concepts. In order for language to work, at least two people have to agree that they have a common experience or concept, and they then have to code the experience with a sound, phrase, or gesture that will represent the concept. For example, if you and I have shared the experience of watching early *Star Trek* episodes, I can say to you, "Beam me up, Scotty," and you will immediately understand that I want to leave this place. Without that common background, you would have no idea what I was talking about, and you would wonder why I wasn't calling you by your correct name.

If I say to you, "Racism is a major problem in our society," you will probably understand that I am referring to a set of negative and discriminatory behaviors based on ethnicity and culture. We have a common understanding of this "code" because we have shared certain social, political, and educational experiences. Regardless of whether you agree with me, you will know what I mean. But if I say to the average American, "Breaker thinking is a major problem of our society," I will probably get a blank stare (unless the person has read this book). The use of code makes no sense without prior agreement based on common experience.

This is as true of nonverbal communication as of verbal. (According to language researchers, the former accounts for 60 to 75 percent of our communication.)

Someone once told me that the coded gesture of raising the thumb in the air with the fist closed, which in our culture means "I agree enthusiastically," in a certain Middle Eastern culture means "Screw you!" He said he learned this the hard way.

There is certainly lack of agreement on how to speak about The Mess. The Center for the American Dream, in their survey of American attitudes toward consumption, values, and security, found that

> people are struggling to find a vocabulary that captures their concerns. Indeed, one obstacle to moving forward on the issue of consumption is language. People share a sense of what the problem is but have trouble agreeing on what to call it.[33]

One purpose of this book is to help provide a common code with which to refer to The Mess and to the emerging society. With a common language, our ability to see and then do something about our predicament increases dramatically.

The Role of Culture

If consciousness is the way we perceive "I" in relationship to "other," culture is the set of behaviors that act out that perception. If I perceive/believe that grasshoppers are food, I will act accordinging to that belief and gather grasshoppers for dinner. To the extent that others believe and do the same thing, we form a "culture."

If I believe that grasshoppers are pests, I will act accordingly and spray them with pesticides. And my children will be raised to see the world that way.

Whether you believe that insects are food or pests, chances are that your belief developed not from your own direct life experience but from what your culture taught you.

By "taught," I do not mean that someone sat down with you and said, "Now, Suzie, this thing is a grasshopper and it is good to eat and this is how you eat it." What happened is that you saw someone eating a grasshopper and imitated her. Alternatively, you found a grasshopper in the yard, stuck it in your mouth, and then found yourself surrounded by adults screaming, yelling, pleading with you to spit it out, and calling the doctor. You had just been "taught" that eating grasshoppers is bad.

If taught that "I" am separate from "you" (whether separate-and-superior or separate-and-inferior), I will develop or accept a set of behaviors through which I can act out that teaching. Exclusivity becomes my culture. This culture is practiced in a million different ways, every day, to the point that I consider it "normal."

Most of our culture is normalizing and encompassing. We don't see our consciousness as an accumulation of the beliefs and perceptions of others—we see "reality." We don't see our behavior as one of a countless number of possible valid actions—we generally don't see our behavior at all. When we encounter those who act differently, we tend to see them as "wrong" or "evil." Even among the "enlightened," encountering another culture means becoming "tolerant" of others; we rarely stop to think that the others are trying to be tolerant of *our* bizarre behaviors!

Your consciousness was shaped by your mother before you had any filters of rational thought—even before you were born. Your behaviors were shaped from the first moments of consciousness, still deep inside the womb. No one ever "taught" you your culture; you have always been surrounded by it. It is difficult to move far enough away to get an objective view of culture. "Story" becomes "reality."

Maintaining the Culture of Exclusivity

A friend related the following experience:

> My mother and father always taught that everyone is equal, and that everyone deserves a fair shake. However, when we

were youngsters in our family car, we would get a different lesson. At a certain point in our journey, my father would say, without turning his head, "Okay, everyone lock up now." We were all supposed to lock the doors to the car. The only thing that was different about that part of our trip was that the people on the streets were black instead of white.

That was a powerful lesson. To this day, I still want to lock my car doors when I see black people on the street, even though I know I'm in no more danger than at the beginning of my journey.

Because of culture, people think their behavior is normal, no matter how eccentric it may appear to others. People defend practices related to death, mutilation, and oppression on the grounds that they are "cultural." The institutions of slavery and segregation were maintained for hundreds of years, each generation being taught that these practices were normal. Similarly, we are currently engaged in behaviors that our grandchildren will consider as barbaric as slavery: clearcutting forests, permitting the virtually unregulated sale of cigarettes, tolterating hunger and homelessness, chemically manufacturing food, keeping people in economic slavery.

While culture maintains behavior, the opposite is also true: behavior maintains culture. Behavior sets up a tendency, a "field," in which it is easier to act within the dictates of culture than it is to operate outside of it. In a culture that eats grasshoppers, it is much easier to go along and eat grasshoppers than to fight the grasshopper eaters. It is easier to act as if conspicuous consumption were important to you, even if it is not. It is easier to live the Breaker story, even when you know it is dysfunctional, than to change it.

As we shall see later, although consciousness and culture are deeply entrenched, they *can* be transformed. In the case of exclusivity, they *must* be changed, for the good of all.

The Role of Psychological Coherence

The Breaker story "hangs together." Thousands of times a day, in schools and colleges, in the workplace and in social institutions, we are reminded how the parts of the Breaker story weave together to form a coherent whole. The story may not be pleasant or even welcome, but it has a logical organization. Every Breaker institution interlocks with every other one. You can see the ramifications of the Breaker story by interacting with it from any direction.

For example, you may own a car. The automobile industry is not self-contained. It depends on the covering of more and more farmland with asphalt and the drilling of ever-deeper wells to extract ever more scarce fossil fuels. It also shares responsibility for the huge annual harvest of death on American roads.

Similarly, education interlocks with commerce, helping to indoctrinate children in the Breaker story. McDonalds and Pizza Hut run concessions in school cafeterias. Corporate commercials punctuate programs shown on closed-circuit educational television. High school sports teams boost the Nike brand name.

We have a tendency to cling to what *seems* to make sense, what appears to be reasonable. The otherwise "normal" people of Germany accepted Nazism in part because the system was made to appear normal. In the United States, when citizens were rounded up and put in concentration camps for the sole "crime" of having Japanese ancestry, few white Americans protested. It was a "reasonable" thing to go along with, especially since the president and other "reasonable" men condoned it. Each citizen who acquiesced in this offense made it easier for others to do so.

Belief and Perception

Do I believe the guy in the business suit and the confident stride is a trustworthy, upstanding individual? Do I believe that he is powerful? If so, my beliefs will create my perception. And my perception will influence the perceptions of others.

What do I believe about our society? That America is the greatest? That we are the world's oldest democracy? (We only started practicing democracy in 1965, with the passage of the Civil Rights Act.) That we are the leaders of the free world? (America has the largest prison population on Earth.) That we are the most prosperous nation? (We have more homeless people per capita than most Third World countries.)

I will see what I believe. If I believe women are weak, I will see a world full of weak women (and a few exceptions). If I believe blacks are mentally inferior, or Japanese are brainy, or whites are powerful, these beliefs will shape the world I see. Anything that does not fit will be considered an exception to the rule. Breaker Society consists of these shaping beliefs. Taken together, they create the Breaker story.

Fallacies of Power and Powerlessness

In order to change the Breaker society, we must first give up our cherished sense of limitation. This includes the notion that we don't have power. Many of us, especially those raised in the shadow of the Sixties, have strongly developed notions of power—for example:

- Only "They" have power.
- Power is bad.
- Power must be fought.

At the dawn of the twenty-first century, all our notions of power and powerlessness must be reexamined.

Only "They" Have Power

A view of reality that places power outside yourself and beyond reach is inherently self-defeating. The analysis itself creates a power vacuum that "They" step in to fill. So the movement toward this fallacy has two steps:

1. The creation of a void on the part of the "powerless."
2. The filling of that void by the "powerful."

This scenario plays itself out in countless ways every single day:

> We may make the assumption that a middle-aged white male walking down the street in a suit and tie with a briefcase is "powerful." In fact, he is most likely a lower-level minion in the Breaker society bureaucracy who does not have the power to blow his own nose without official approval. He may even be broke and looking for a job, the only thing in his briefcase a copy of *Employment Weekly*.
>
> The secretaries looking at him create the illusion of his power. The homeless street person with hand stretched out for quarters creates the illusion of his power. The punk rockers dressed in black looking disparagingly at "the suit" create his illusion of power. You create the illusion of his power. But the illusion never becomes reality: this man is never powerful. It's just that everyone, himself included, thinks he is.

"Only 'They' have power" also means that whoever you see as having power over your life is your enemy. You are caught in a classic and irreconcilable love–hate relationship: "They" have power over your life, so you need them to take care of you. At the same time, you want to be free of coercion and control, so you resist the power "They" have over you.

The person you have created as your enemy may in fact be your friend, may be just as powerless (or powerful) as you, may have your best interests at heart, but the power fallacy prevents you from seeing any of this.

Power Is Bad

The root of this notion lies in an oft-misquoted statement by the nineteenth-century English historian Lord Acton: "Power *tends to* corrupt and absolute power corrupts absolutely"[34] (emphasis mine).

In reality, power is a tool, like fire. Power is as bad or corrupt as fire. Power is as good, beneficial, and necessary as fire. Humans have used fire for evil, corrupt purposes (arson), as a means of punishment (burning at the stake), and thoughtlessly (the cigarette butt that causes a forest fire). Fire has also been used as a valuable tool for human advancement and culture (warming, cooking, waste treatment, artistic creation, technology).

Fire is amoral. And so is power. We can speak of morality only in regard to how and why they are used.

The same is true of the Breaker story. We will have a world that works for all when we can use exclusivity as we use fire: in a controlled, deliberate way to achieve a specific purpose. Fire that is out of control is usually bad for all beings. So are Breakers who are out of control.

Power Must Be Fought

Fighting power is the behavior that keeps negative attitudes regarding power entrenched. Being in perpetual attack mode fuels the crises that justify further attack. Fighting power creates the *necessity* of fighting power.

Fighting power also guarantees that you will forever be without power. If any in your group gain a measure of power, those former friends will immediately become the new "They," the new focus of hostility. (The only way they could have gained power is by "selling out.")

The Power Drive

The desire to have and use power is pretty basic to our nature and the nature of all species. We will not have a successful Mender society without taking our power issues into consideration, any more than if we tried to ignore or suppress our sexual drives or our need for food.

However, there is a difference between the appropriate use of power and an addiction to power. Billionaires who never cease in their quest for greater success are really trying to get not more money but more control. Their story is "Creating a World Controlled by Me." Breakers not only don't trust natural processes, they don't trust any process they do not personally control.

An excessive need to control is symptomatic of a fundamental lack of faith.

> *Though I do not believe*
> *that a plant will spring up*
> *where no seed has been,*
> *I have great faith in a seed.*
> *Convince me that you have a seed there,*
> *and I am prepared to expect wonders.*
>
> —HENRY DAVID THOREAU[35]

Do I have faith in natural processes? I'm learning. Trust means understanding the natural process, then moving in concert with it. I am learning to plant seeds and wait for fruit.

In Savannah, Georgia, people built houses with the main portion ten feet off the ground and wooden shutters on the windows. They had "faith" that the hurricanes would come. Nowadays, people put their beachfront houses right on the shoreline, daring the waves to come—which they always do. Or they perch their houses on mud-covered hills because they believe they can exempt themselves from the laws of gravity through engineering.

Because human control of the environment is always partial at best, Breakers can never be satisfied, can never experience having their hunger fed and their safety guaranteed. They remain forever empty, searching for that which cannot be found.

Keepers are satisfied because they know that they are not in conscious control. Breakers are unsatisfied because they strive to be in total control, yet deep inside realize that such control is not attainable. Menders are satisfied because, although we know how to control and manipulate, *we don't have to.* We have faith that most things can operate just fine without human intervention. Menders exercise control only to correct Breakers' destabilizing tendencies and achieve a decent life for all.

How Stories Change

If our story is inappropriate and dysfunctional, does that mean we are stuck with it?

Up to this point, we have seen how difficult it is for stories to change, the ways our culture, consciousness, and external conditions combine to create an unshakably coherent world.

However, stories do change. Now that we have examined the conditions under which stories remain the same, let us now turn to the five key factors that can transform the Breaker Story. Those five factors are

- A Change in External Conditions
- An Appeal to the Heart
- An Appeal to Reason
- A Promise of a Better Life
- An Appeal to the Transcendent

A Change in External Conditions

The environment for a story can change. If the change is very subtle, the story may continue in a slightly modified form. However, if the external change is large or profound, the story must shift to accommodate it. Examples range from major climatic changes to the appearance of inventions that transform daily life.

An Appeal to the Heart

There are times when stories change because the force of moral persuasion changes our values and our behavior. Through the awakening of compassion, we come to see our existing life, our present story, as inadequate.

Powerful examples of this appeal to the heart include

- The prophetic/messianic messages of visionaries such as Lao Tzu, Moses, Jesus, Buddha, and Muhammad, who attempted to consciously change our stories by appealing to what is best within us.
- Gandhi's movement for independence in India.
- Martin Luther King's movement for civil and human rights in America.
- Václav Havel's "Velvet Revolution" in Czechoslovakia.
- Desmond Tutu's "Rainbow People" nonviolent movement in South Africa.

An Appeal to Reason

Stories may also change as a result of new understanding. A story is a way of choosing to see the world. The appeal to reason asks us to think carefully and revise our view.

An example of the appeal to reason was the economic, political, and historical analysis of Karl Marx. Marx wove together compelling arguments (from the point of view of exploited workers) for the dismantling of the capitalist system.

A Promise of a Better Life

One of the most powerful influences on stories is an emerging conviction among people that their lives can be better. Whether the underlying drive is the desire to be free from oppressive conditions or the yearning for a more meaningful life, the promise of improvement lies at the heart of virtually all attempts at changing story.

In some instances, the better life is promised not here but in the hereafter. If that is the case, the new story may do little to weaken the hold of present oppression.

An Appeal to the Transcendent

Stories change when people are asked to consider lives other than their own. Moving beyond "What's in it for me?" opens us to a story larger than what Peter Russell calls our "skin-encapsulated ego." Transcending the personal self can come in many ways:

- Through identification with one's tribe, clan, community, or nation—or with the entire human family.
- Through an awareness of an ecological, interspecies reality. "Save the whales," for example, is a slogan inviting us to look beyond our anthropocentric, ecologically damaging stories.
- Through a consciousness of the hereafter. Contemplation of spirits, ancestors, and guides may help us to reexamine our present story.

Of the five story-changing influences just discussed, which can we depend on to promote the desired shift from the Breaker story to the Mender story? Answer: all of them. Through a combination of external forces for change, an internal longing for a better world, and appeals to our reason, our compassion, and our spirit, we will move our society from its present deadly course and toward a world that works for all.

PART THREE

THE REVOLUTION
TO INCLUSIVITY

What is hope? It is the presentiment that imagination is more real and reality is less real than it looks. It is the hunch that the overwhelming brutality of facts that oppress and repress are not the last word. It is the suspicion that reality is more complex than realism wants us to believe; that the frontiers of the possible are not determined by the limits of the actual, and that in a miraculous and unexpected way, life is preparing the creative events which will open the way to freedom and resurrection.

—RUBEM ALVES[36]

IN SOME MIRACULOUS and mysterious sense, we are living at the dawn of a new era of human liberation—liberation from our own foolish notions of how the world works.

Part Three shows how we can cooperate with this emerging change. Chapter 7 is about the change in our consciousness: the internal revolution. Chapter 8 is about the change in our culture and institutions: the external revolution. And finally, in the Conclusion, we come to the most important aspect of our transformation: our commitment to make it happen.

7

The Internal Revolution— Feeding Your Internal Hunger

How do we get to the bottom of our delusions of separation? How do we tame the Breaker story within? How do we develop the courage to face The Other—within ourselves? How can we learn to be compassionate with ourselves, and then extend that compassion to others?

Work for the World and Develop Yourself

For Menders, there is a dual purpose in our activism: to transform ourselves and to transform our world. Either one, by itself, is not enough.

I can work on myself by attending a continual round of self-help workshops and seminars. This is egocentric, self-indulgent, and an example of "New Age" Breaker thinking. Or I can work on myself by working to help others. Putting the needs of others (including the Earth) first is the way I can heal the worst effects of Breaker culture, both within myself and in the world at large. However, working for others, without clarifying the limitations and boundaries of my heart, can also be egocentric and self-indulgent.

THE SWORD AND THE PATH

The people of a mythical Olde Towne find it necessary to cut a path to a New Town. Some residents are sharpening their long swords. Each edge is already finely sharpened, but still they hone them. Each day, they are at their wheels, grinding away at their blades, refining their swords ever further. After they get their blades to a microscopic sharpness, they sharpen even further. To the suggestion that they actually use their swords to cut a path to the New Town, they reply: "We're not ready. Our swords are not sharp enough yet!"

In another place in the Olde Towne, another group of people is actually blazing a path to the New Town. They are hacking through the underbrush. It's slow, tedious, dangerous, mainly because their cutting blades are dull, rusted, and in some instances even broken. Many people tear at the underbrush with their bare, bleeding hands. They curse the slow going, the torturous pace. To the suggestion that they take a little time to sharpen their swords, some say, "What swords?" Others protest: "What good would that do? Anyway, this job is too important to take the time to sharpen our blades!"

The sword in this story is the heart. The path in the story is the way to a Mender society. The sword-sharpeners attend every workshop and retreat, purchase every new self-help book, learn whatever mantra is currently being touted, all in an effort to sharpen the already fine edge of their hearts. They give little thought to what a well-honed heart might be *for*. Those who ignore our responsibility to create a world that works for all fall easily into the self-absorption and "holier-than-thou" attitudes of exclusivity.

Those on the "path," such as social activists and environmentalists, have dedicated their lives to changing the existing system.

They spend their days attacking the system, protesting injustices, fighting for social, environmental, and other causes. They have not seen that the principal tool to produce that change, compassion, must be refined if it is to be capable of performing its task. Many are motivated more by anger at what is wrong than expectant joy at what could be right. If they actually get to the new town, it will look to them a lot like the one they have left behind, for they carry the spirit of Old Towne in their hearts.

This chapter is about sharpening the sword. The following one is about cutting the path.

Activism as a Spiritual Discipline

Being a Mender, an activist for an inclusive society, is a spiritual discipline. We practice a different kind of spirituality: the spirituality of turbulent times. Working to alleviate suffering is the way we practice our faith. We try not to act from anger or fear. We act because, in this life we have been given, we believe we can help make things better.

Acting out of our compassion to lessen suffering and improve the lives of others is the way we celebrate the Spirit. Knowing that each of our acts, however small, builds the vitality of the Web of Life brings us joy, satisfaction, and power.

In the Spirit-driven model, it doesn't matter whether a person is "successful" in changing the condition. While practical goals are important, the spiritual goal is to awaken the compassion that lies at the root of all change. "Success" doesn't mean I've saved an endangered species or cleaned up a toxic waste dump or fed hungry children. Success means awakening in myself a Spirit that can help make a better life for others. Success means I have acted in the world as though I were a part of it, not apart from it. Success means becoming conscious of and faithful to my values and to my soul.

Success and Destiny

An ordinary man, thin, in shirtsleeves, shopping bags in hand, walks down a main street in a large city on a sunny day. Just a nameless, faceless part of the crowd. An ordinary man, perfectly poised in a moment in history to give us a powerful image of courage and commitment, perfectly poised to show the world what one person can do in the face of apparently overwhelming odds. One man who graphically represents The Power of One.

All he does is step off the sidewalk and stop a tank.

Think about the confluence of events. Is this the first time he has ever seen a column of tanks? What is it about this particular day, this particular tank column, this particular street corner, that causes him to step off the curb and into the tank's path? His "success" is not that he permanently stops the tanks. He doesn't. His success is that his act awakens many people around the world to the transformative power of one committed person.

Think about the tank commander—what makes him stop? Is it the sight of courage in the form of a single small person? Is it the student's frailty in the face of mechanized might? Is it the commander's own personal doubts about the morality of his mission?

Consider the photographer, operating his video equipment from the roof of a nearby building. Why is he set up at precisely that spot, at precisely that angle, ready to shoot an image that will go down in history? Is there an intuition, a hunch, of his destined historic role?

We know, of course, that the hero of Tiananmen Square gave his life because he stood for his convictions. What is less known is that the tank commander was also executed—for doubting his convictions.

As for the photographer, does he lie awake at night, questioning whether or not those images caused the deaths of those two men? What would have happened had he not recorded the incident, had he not made the images available for broadcast around the world—images that embarrassed an already provoked government?

Like these three individuals, each of us is perfectly poised to fulfill our moment of destiny. The circumstances of our birth, our life experiences, education, emotional traumas, the "chance" occurrence of being at a certain place at a certain time—these are the raw materials of a larger and mysterious providence.

It Does Not Matter What Your Chances Are

Being Spirit-driven means acting in the face of overwhelming odds. Confronted by the challenge, we cannot refrain from action. It is precisely our willingness to tackle the impossible that makes radical change possible.

> *Just because I'm outnumbered doesn't mean I'm wrong.*
> —MOIRA GUNN[37]

Years ago, a reporter asked then Soviet president Mikhail Gorbachev what he thought his chances were of reforming Soviet society through perestroika. Gorbachev replied that even thinking about chances was self-defeating. "What choice do we have?" he asked the reporter. He went on to say that a man dropped in the middle of the ocean will start swimming to one shore or another, not refuse to swim because of the magnitude of the task ahead of him.

The Breaker society looks formidable. In many ways, it is. But can we afford not to make the changes?

The Three Practices of a Mender

What attitudes, beliefs, and hopes will form the building blocks of the Mender society? What is it that will feed our hunger for the sacred?

Three practices will help us develop the quality of consciousness that Keepers take for granted:

- Practicing Enoughness
- Practicing Inclusive Compassion
- Reconnecting with Our Relationships

Practicing Enoughness

We live in a society either scarred by scarcity or spoiled by luxury. We have no idea how much is *enough*. We don't know when to quit. A key to dismantling exclusivity within yourself is to know how much is enough. Your answer to the question "How much is enough?" will depend on the story you are enacting.[38]

Breakers—There Is Never Enough

The Breaker Society rests on a premise: there is not enough (of anything) for all. The world is a place of limitation. Therefore, you have to work to get "enough" for yourself. This usually means doing something that directly or indirectly takes resources from others. Since there is not enough, getting "more" provides greater security against times of lack.

Keepers—The Earth Is Abundant

Keepers, and all other beings, start from a radically different premise: the Earth is incredibly abundant. All humans need to do is be receptive to the abundance. Because the Earth is abundant, because there is always another gazelle, it is not necessary to try to get "more." There is always enough.

Keepers know that the universe always provides. Included in this provision are the knowledge, skills, and abilities to obtain whatever we need. The universe does not kill the gazelle, skin it, and put it in our stewpot. The universe provides the gazelle, and also our ability to catch it, clean it, and cook it. Taking the action is up to us.

Menders—Abundance Needs Our Help

Menders accept the premise that the Earth is abundant, but recognize that her systems have been stressed to the limit by Breaker greed and fear of lack. These systems need to come back into balance before we can rely again on the Earth's own balancing act. Menders will catalyze that balance. For Menders, "enough" means that all wants, needs, and wishes are satisfied within the context of a healing and regenerating global ecosystem.

> Assume you are the leader of a tribe of eight hundred people. You are meeting with the head of another tribe, also with eight hundred people. You are discussing a well that is large enough to reliably and sustainably supply water to about two thousand people per day.
>
> This is a win/win/win scenario. Both tribes can win, and so can the world, without taxing the regenerative capacity of the well.
>
> What if the leader of the other tribe decides he wants all of the water? He wants to bottle the "excess" and sell to other tribes, including yours. He also wants the right to expand his tribe and keep all of the water. He has guns.
>
> Instantly, your two tribes are in conflict. The conflict is not one of resources. The amount of water in the well has not changed. The problem is not a lack of water but a clash of concepts. Your concept of "enoughness" is obviously in conflict with his.
>
> He threatens to go to war over the issue. What do you do? What are your choices?

To develop an understanding of what might be enough for us, we must first be clear about all of the ways we can possibly be filled—and conversely, all of the ways we can be empty. The areas we will need to take into account (some of them overlapping) are:

Physical/material
Food and water
Shelter
Clothing

Emotional
Love
Caring
Respect
Touch
Purpose
Safety
Joy/happiness
Sorrow/grief

Mental
Education
Intellectual stimulation
Meaning

Social
Family
Community
Nation
Tribe
Service/sacrifice

Transcendent
Peace
Beauty
Bliss
Meditation/contemplation
Devotional service
Ceremony and ritual
Creativity

Other
Reproduction
Work
Recreation

My emptiness is filled when *all* my empty spaces receive what they need. This is the basis of "enoughness."

If you look deeply into your emptiness, you will find that it is chambered. Think of it as a car battery. Filling one chamber will not make it work. Overfilling one chamber will not make it work. While Breaker leaders try to keep us focused on the material chamber, Menders know that all chambers must be filled. Our challenge is to make sure that each and every chamber in each and every one of us has "enough."

Overfilling one person or group does not create a society of fulfillment or enoughness.

- The fact that one's community includes individuals wealthy enough to support a symphony or a yacht club means nothing to a homeless and hungry person.

- A community that has one millionaire CEO and nine impoverished families may have an average annual household income of $100,000. Does such a statistic have any meaning?
- Obesity is the result of trying to fill all of one's emptiness with food. The futility of this effort is painfully obvious.

Steps Toward Enoughness

- *Know how much is enough for yourself.* For example, based on the example of other professionals, I have established a maximum salary for myself. (That maximum is related to median salary ranges in my locale.) If the maximum is ever reached in any given year, I am committed to keeping my earnings at that level, deferring the excess to another year, or giving 100 percent of it away. While currently living quite comfortably on less than half of my maximum, it is good to know when I will be getting off the acquisition bus.

- *Be aware of your own excessiveness.* Do you want more money every year because you need it or because "everybody else is getting it"? Do you see money as a measure of your worth as a person? Do you really want and need what you are buying?

- *Discuss with others your respective notions of "enough."* Many of us think that the spending and lifestyles of those we see as "super-rich" are excessive but find it difficult to articulate what is "enough" for ourselves. Discussion on this subject in your community will help to clarify your ideas.

- *Pay attention to all your "chambers."* When you recognize "enoughness" in one chamber, examine what is happening in the others. If you have "enough" shelter, start filling the creativity or service chamber.

- *Become conscious of where your money is going.* You support the Breaker society economically. So do I. It's pretty hard not to. The pervasiveness of the Breaker consciousness means that the natural abundance and resources of our planet go to Breaker maintenance and support. The most we can do in this transition time is to support it less.

Questions about money reveal some of our deepest attitudes. Do you believe that "money" is something dirty, evil, better left alone? Do you believe it is your birthright? A burden you must bear? Your just reward for hard work? A natural accompaniment of your status? Do you believe that people with money are inherently bad? Inherently good? Inherently powerful? Do you believe there is such a thing as "enough" money?

A few years ago, my finances were so bad that I went to Beatrice, a noted Portland astrologer, for help. She told me: "Money is a being, like a person. Assuming that this is true, what is your relationship with that being called Money?"

I laughed out loud. "If money were a woman, she'd leave me for all of the bad things that I say about her!" I started to tick off on my fingers my common complaints about money:

- You're never there when I need you.
- I can't rely on you.
- You hang out with all the wrong people.
- There's never enough of you.
- You don't really love me.
- You don't support me.

I finished my litany with "No wonder money doesn't stick around!" And since that time, my relationship with money has changed to one of mutual respect and abundance—not seven figures, but comfortable enough for my simple lifestyle.

Practicing Inclusive Compassion

Compassion is a grace, not an achievement. Its constancy does not ultimately depend upon an effort of will, but upon a relationship to the Spirit.

—MARCUS BORG[39]

Compassion is love's verb. Webster's dictionary says that compassion is a noun, and as we all know from grade school, a noun is a "person, place, or thing." I think Noah Webster was wrong. I think compassion is the verb of love. Beyond saying "I love you," how do we love? How do we act out our love in the world? Through compassion.

Compassion is not taught; it is awakened. Everyone has the capacity for compassion, just as every healthy newborn has the capacity to draw breath. Like the newborn, our compassion may need the assistance of a slap on the butt, but that only jump-starts what is innate.

I needed the slap on the butt. I was not born into a family or a community that regularly practiced compassion. Compassion is something that was awakened in me relatively late in life. It is something I have to think about, pay attention to, cultivate.

It is relatively easy for me to be compassionate with the lovable—those who smile at me, those who react to me out of love and concern. It is much harder to be compassionate with the *apparently* unlovable.

Compassion as Attention

I believe it was the French religious philosopher Simone Weil who wrote, "Prayer is paying attention." Attention is also one of the indicators of compassion. It is listening, but listening with more than just the ear. Attention is whole-body listening. There is a saying from an ancient Chinese text that a chicken hatches her egg by mentally listening to it.[40] She gives all of her attention, all her being, to that egg, thereby creating the energy, the heat that hatches it. (In Breaker thought, this is a folk tale; only physical heat, something that is measurable, is responsible for eggs hatching.)

To whom do you give your attention? It is a sad and strange by-product of exclusivity that most of the "people" who receive our attention are not humans at all but little electronic blips in a cathode ray tube. We have substituted television talk-show hosts for our flesh-and-blood intimates.

When the average urbanite is invited to be compassionate, to attend to another human being who is living on the street, the typical response is to turn away from the potential encounter. The reason? "That person might hurt me." But it is as if we feared any reaction from the other, not just a painful one. Television and movies have taught us that "safe" intimacy is nonreactive. We cry during *Terms of Endearment* or *Touched by an Angel* (or even *E.T.*), but do those characters on the screen see our tears? React to them? Television provides the safe alternative to intimacy, a false intimacy that allows us to have feelings toward total strangers as long as there are no consequences. The ultimate in risk-free interactions is over the Internet. The anonymity of chat rooms relieves us of the obligation to truly attend to another.

Even though we may profess to love others, what we do with others in real life is a different story. Years ago, at a psychology conference in San Diego, attendees at the plenary sessions were singing wonderful New Age songs, swaying back and forth, holding hands, openly expressing their love for each other. Many of them would then leave the conference room and treat the mainly Latino busboys and university staff like dirt. They would walk right by them, not make eye contact, not thank them or acknowledge them as human. The people wearing the conference tags were human; others were just furniture, to be used or ignored according to convenience.

That ignoring, that ignorance, causes all hearts to shrivel up. When you ignore another person, it puts calluses on your heart and starves the heart of the other. Even compassion, when practiced without true connection, can have this effect—for example, dropping coins in a cup without looking at the person holding the cup, giving money to a charity without interacting with the beneficiaries. The poor in spirit need not only our food or shelter, they need our attention.

Incidentally, ignorance of this kind is a primary complaint about the "racism" of whites toward people of color. Black America has been crying out for recognition of the pain inflicted by the history of slavery and oppression. However, the issue here isn't really racism; it is something far more insidious. It is a failure to *attend*. It is a failure of compassion.

Our ignorance, our failure to attend, create the environment of hardheartedness and sociopathic symptoms that we spend billions of dollars trying to control. But look at how we try to control that behavior. With further isolation, further withdrawal of attention, further deprivation of touch and attention. With prisons, reform schools, mental institutions, ghettos. (Or gated subdivisions, regional malls, elitist country clubs, private schools.) Our attempts at control in a society that suffers from a lack of compassion are pouring buckets of gasoline on an already blazing fire.

If people don't get positive attention, they will try for negative attention. *Any* attention is better than no attention at all.

Look at the ways we try to fill our hunger for attention, whether positive or negative. If we are middle-class, we may overspend our budgets in the pursuit of an "upwardly mobile" lifestyle. If rich, we may try to buy love and attention through politics, support for the arts, or the creation of an entourage of "groupies" (either adoring fans or fawning corporate vice presidents). If lower-class, our attempts to gain attention may take the form of militant posturing, acting tough and angry with the world. And no matter what our class, we may turn to various drugs of choice, from cheap wine to cocaine to Valium, for a hollow semblance of attention. We can *feel* loved, even if the feeling is only chemically induced. (All such actions appear desperate and meaningless to those who do not experience this particular kind of deprivation. The guy from the ghetto wearing tiers of gold chains and a neck-lace of beepers looks ridiculous to the middle-class family man. And Mr. Middle Class going into debt to join a country club looks stupid to Mr. Beepers.)

Compassion as Awareness of Suffering

Through our compassion, we can attend to the suffering of others. We can feel the pain of a woman paying for her groceries in food stamps as the clerk and other shoppers look on in scorn. We can feel the pain of someone who, despite his material "success," con-stantly struggles with feelings of inadequacy as a man. We can per-ceive the painful bewilderment of a youth who has been constantly entertained, to the point that he does not understand the purpose of life.

In order to help another, we have to let go of our own cher-ished prejudices concerning limitation, suffering, and pain. We have to let go of middle-class rationalizations like

- They deserve what they're getting.
- They don't really want any better.
- They like living like that.

. . . or any of the other concepts we use to ignore the pain of others. Similarly, we have to release ourselves of lower-class ratio-nalizations like

- They deserve what they're getting *(if it's bad)*.
- They don't deserve what they're getting *(if it's good)*.
- I'm justified in expressing my anger this way.
- They have been stealing from my people, so it's
  okay to steal from them.

A Journey Toward Compassion

Years ago, on awakening one morning, these words came to me: "The foundation and primary motivation for the revolution to an authentic society is LOVE AND COMPASSION."

Real simple. We just get everyone to love everyone else, and all other beings, and then we can all go home.

The only problem with that simple formula is that no one wants to put it into practice. (Or at least, the number of people I see actually practicing unconditional love and compassion can be counted on the fingers of my two hands—with a few fingers left over.) We all practice, at best, conditional compassion: I will be compassionate with those I choose; the others can wait, perhaps forever.

We all have our arguments on why compassion won't work, or how it's impractical under the circumstances, how the "other guy" has to be compassionate first, how he doesn't really want, deserve, or need our compassion. Or, worst of all, how we are already being compassionate to him.

Compassion is a state of being that is attached to perception. I can feel at one only with those I can see. My personal upbringing allows me to be very compassionate toward those who lack the basic resources of life: food, clothing, shelter. I find it more difficult to be compassionate toward people who are in emotional pain yet have material affluence. But I have come to realize that their lives are no less painful, only different.

Perhaps the statement above should be modified to say I can feel at one only with those I choose to see. Over the past two decades, and for reasons I don't fully understand, I have chosen to extend my perception—and hence my compassion—to those who are very different from me, whether they are people or other kinds of beings. This has given me a perspective from which I can be compassionate with both hunter and hunted, killer and victim, the forest and those who would destroy it.

My problem is, How do I invite others to share that perspective? How do I ask someone to let go of his or her accustomed focus and encompass a wider reality beyond the judgment of duality? How do I invite people to the common ground?

When I invite people of color to the common ground, I am called an Uncle Tom and an apologist for white racism. When I invite whites to the common ground, I am called a black national-ist and reverse racist. When I invite environmentalists to the com-mon ground, I am accused of being pro-timber and pro-industry; when I invite loggers, I am accused of being an environmentalist.

Regardless of these initial accusations, I continue in my work, for the rewards are great. Once people venture on to the common ground, they frequently let go of their suspicions and learn to see the world from an inclusive perspective. And suddenly I no longer appear naive!

What were the mechanisms that caused a skinny colored kid from Camden, New Jersey, to adopt a philosophy of love for both victims and villains?

It really has been a mysterious process for me. I didn't wake up one day and decide to love the rest of the world. It had little to do with formal religion. There were no earth-shaking personal expe-riences that catapulted me into a deeper awareness or knowing. It was simply a very quiet Blessing that has been growing in me for some time.

Think about the words of the hymn revered by Christians everywhere:

> *Amazing Grace! How sweet the sound*
> *that saved a wretch like me.*
> *I once was lost and now I'm found,*
> *was blind and now I see.*

Locked in the pain and anguish of a meaningless life in a brutal environment, I was indeed blind. My partial blindness skewed my vision, caused me to look at the world a certain way, seeing "ene-mies." My behavior was appropriate to one who is blind.

At some point in time, through the Grace of an ever merciful and very patient Creator, my inner eyes opened. At least part way.

Love. Compassion. Forgiveness. These are all words that were drilled into us in Sunday School (or Saturday School, or whenever our particular religion did its teaching). If these are to become more than words, we need to ask for Grace and be open to it when it comes into our lives. Since The Other may be the bearer of Grace, to deny The Other is to deny God.

Seeing the Wounded Child

In *Being Peace,* Thich Nhat Hanh writes about the dangers of piracy in the South China Sea during the exodus of boat people from Vietnam.[41] Pirates in that area would board the refugee boats, steal all the valuables, rape the women, and kill the men. Hanh says that it's easy to be compassionate toward the twelve-year-old girl who is raped and murdered by pirates; it's very difficult to be compassionate toward the pirate.

Hanh suggests that if we look at the pirate as the wounded child that he is, and at that child's life experiences and environment, we will begin to feel his terrible pain and to glimpse how he could have developed such a hardness of heart that he could commit an act like the rape and murder of a young girl. The pirate was not born a monster. Hanh suggests connecting with the human being that preceded the monster. It's not easy.

When you look at that child, look through all the armoring and negativity he puts in front of you. Then you can really reach him with your compassion.

I was the only person in the room not packing an automatic pistol.

I was doing a series of trainings with police officers from small towns. There were a dozen uniformed officers in the small training room. All of them were muscular, and half were wearing bulletproof vests, which made them appear even larger. One sat at the table opposite me. He had a buzz haircut, carefully folded hands, and the steady gaze cops use to intimidate suspects. After taking a few deep breaths, using Thich Nhat Hanh's suggestion, I looked at him as an interesting eight-year-old I wanted to get to know.

Officer Buzzcut did not move a muscle for the first hour of the training, never let up on the intense "cop stare." After an hour, he raised his hand and, without smiling or altering his gaze, said: "I just want you to know I'm getting a lot out of this training. I really feel welcome here. I've been to other trainings that really didn't treat us as human beings with feelings. I would really get my feelings hurt in those sessions, but we are trained not to say anything back to the trainers. You are really treating us like human beings and I appreciate it."

The boots, guns, clubs, uniforms are just a mask, a shield, a persona. They are just a way of trying to hide the wounded, damaged child (and a way of meeting the requirements of a Breaker system that equates fear with respect). To look through all of that, to see the child behind the uniform, to see the child with low self-esteem who was put down by his parents, ridiculed by others, is to help the man become a fully functioning human, no longer needing to take out his pain on others.

The Risks of Compassion

What risks do we take in being compassionate?

- The risk that we will be rejected and unloved.
- The risk that others may have another agenda.
  Worse yet, they may force their agenda onto us.
- The risk that we will be unheard. This causes us to stay with the groups that agree with us. The feedback loop becomes self-promoting, self-reinforcing, and ultimately self-defeating.

Thich Nhat Hanh encourages us to act despite the risks involved. In the situation with the police officers, my bodily risk was low: they were not going to shoot me or arrest me. The risk was to my ego—a much less substantial but more potent threat. My fear was of being rejected or ignored. But I determined some time ago to take the risk to my ego if that risk could help make the world a better place.

Compassion as the Call to Action

Someone said that our "calling" is the place where our deepest joy intersects with the deepest needs of the Earth. I add a further definition: our calling is the place where our inner joy and our inner terror meet. Our calling is our place of both joy and sacrifice. What risk are the Earth and her families asking of us? I love speaking to groups, but I also experience a moment of terror every time I do so. Where is *your* terror? There lies the direction of your compassion.

The Chinese student who placed himself in front of the line of tanks trying to enter Tiananmen Square was fulfilling a calling. Defying a column of tanks with nothing but your body and a shopping bag is a deep response to the call to compassionate action. This man's actions were powerful precisely because they were nonviolent and nonthreatening. He did not deny the power of the tank commander to run him down; his action expressed the fact that power over his life was simply not as important to him as freedom from oppression.

This same calling led a handful of black students in Greensboro, North Carolina, to sit down at a Woolworth's lunch counter three decades ago to order a Coke, defying the immoral system of American apartheid. The calling led Rosa Parks to defy that same apartheid in her own small but profound way—by simply sitting down in a bus. The calling led Mohandas Gandhi, Martin Luther King, Jr., Nelson Mandela, Václav Havel, and Aung San Suu Kyi to prison for the crime of believing that their nations could be more just than they were.

Compassion and the Chronic Crisis

Over and over, we humans have proven that we are generous and self-sacrificing, and that we will respond compassionately and effectively to a crisis—at least, to an immediate crisis. If there is an earthquake, you will see people risking their lives pulling total strangers out of the wreckage of fallen buildings. When the Willamette River rose to dangerous levels in Portland, Oregon, in 1996, so many thousands of volunteers turned out to help sandbag the river banks, disaster officials had to send many of them home. If there is a plane crash, local hospitals are flooded with healthy people with sleeves rolled up, ready to give blood.

That is what happens in an acute crisis. But what happens in a crisis that builds at a glacial pace? Nothing happens. The Breaker media, geared to sudden catastrophe, do little more than nod to the chronic crisis. People may get concerned, but they do not sustain the concern. Public attention, focused on the immediate, turns to something else, almost anything else. The long-drawn-out crisis continues.

Most of the components of The Mess listed in Chapter 2 are chronic crises that the public is largely unable to react to. We *know* about them, we may be concerned with them, but we seem incapable of doing anything about them. The crises that are killing us have been decades, even centuries, in the making. We need to make visible our chronic crises and sensitize our hearts to them.

Reconnecting with Our Relationships

Reconnecting with Yourself

> A while ago, I was invited by a friend to attend a gathering of Buddhists outside San Francisco. It was a beautiful Sunday. The gathering was held in a white open-air tent, giving a translucent cast to the day. Inside, a monk was delivering the dharma talk in a droning voice; more than a few of the participants were dozing.

At one point, the monk stopped his talk and asked the group, "Who are you?" He then paused for a second and followed up with "What do you want?" He then continued where he had left off with his talk. A few minutes later, he interrupted his talk again with the same two questions: "Who are you?" (Pause.) "What do you want?"

By the third or fourth time, I found my irritation growing. It arose from my great difficulty in coming up with answers to those two simple questions. My reaction was typical: shoot the messenger.

These questions are like a Zen koan, which has no absolute, rational answer. It is the questions themselves, not the answers they may yield, that are of value in our search for self-connection.

These are *ultimate questions* that have formed the basis of my personal quest to reconnect with myself. They have been my pathway to my soul's depth, and I will spend the rest of my life wrestling with them. They are now regularly incorporated into my talks with students, professionals, and others who are so busy with the details of "life" they do not take the time to ask who is living it.

Reconnecting with Place

Breakers don't acknowledge the importance of belonging to a particular place. They even consider that notion "old-fashioned." By contrast, Menders consciously build a relationship with a piece of the Earth, setting down roots and nurturing them.

Whether or not they are mobile—and they certainly have been in this century—Breakers are detached from place. The consciousness that paves over a stream, clearcuts a forest, turns a river into a sewer, or levels an entire mountain for a pick-up truck's worth of gold is a consciousness disconnected from the importance of place.

For Menders, reconnection to place means living in conscious relationship with the local ecosystem and maintaining a concerned awareness of the global one. Like Keepers, Menders see each place on Earth as unique, with its own spiritual vibration, ecology, and healing powers.

The Chinese art of feng shui embodies recognition of the importance of place. Feng shui is the art of placement, suggesting how elements might be best arranged in a landscape, a building, a room. Each location is considered to have a particular quality of energy, which can be enhanced by paying attention to the correct relationships between the elements.

For Breakers, one place is pretty much like another. This truth is evident in Breaker architecture. Aside from the notable skylines of New York and San Francisco, most of our cities are indistinguishable from one another. When shopping downtown or at the mall, would you know whether you were in Houston, Seattle, or Minneapolis? The residential landscape is even more uniform.

In Breaker society, place loses its significance. Breakers never seem to understand why Keepers go nuts when their homes are taken or when the burial sites of their ancestors are disturbed. "We gave them more land some miles away. Why aren't they happy?"

Keepers do not just connect with place. Keepers *are* place. Their identity is as inextricably tied to place as our personal identity is tied to face.

Admittedly, Keepers' identification with place is limiting. Keepers cannot move from one area to another without experiencing dismemberment. They cannot explore outside of their area, because that area is their universe. They are great at understanding the importance of place and adapting themselves to its conditions, but not at changing those conditions. By contrast, Breakers are great at transforming place, even moving mountains and draining rivers to do it, but they are poor at understanding the deeper significance of what they have done.

Menders are learning both how to adapt themselves to place and how to adapt place to their needs. They are developing the talents to make significant, healing, and sustainable changes.

Author Wendell Berry said that not only must we really get to know a place but the place must really get to know *us*. Place is a being. Place, and all of the beings within it, can develop an intimate knowledge of us.

> Years ago, I was driving in Lancaster County, Pennsylvania, the home of the Amish community. It was a cool day, and the fog in the air gave a feeling of otherworldliness to the scene.
>
> As I paused to watch an Amish farmer plant his crop using a horse-drawn plow, it suddenly came to me that the scene before me—farmer, field, horse, plow, seed—was timeless. If my car were a time machine and I traveled back two hundred years, I would see the almost identical ancestors of this farmer, this horse, this seed. If my time machine worked in the other direction, I would see their descendants. The place knows these beings.

Place is one means by which Keepers connect with their ancestors. For Breakers, generally, dead is dead.

Keepers don't merely *believe* in an afterlife; they act as though the departed were an integral part of their everyday lives. One of my Native American friends would constantly interject into our conversations advice he had received from his grandmother. "Grandma said I should take that new job." "Grandma doesn't want me to take that trip—she doesn't want me to be away that long." It was a full three years before I realized that his grandmother was not among the living. Even when I mentioned one day that I would like to meet her, his response was "Sure." (He was planning to take me to her gravesite.)

Your Place in the Natural World

> In Washington, D.C., there are two museums side by side on the Mall: the Museum of American History, which has displays about white people, and the Museum of Natural History, which

covers animals, plants, Eskimos, and Indians (who are clearly not "American" enough to go in the first museum). They would be better named "The Breaker Museum" and "The Keeper Museum."

Connecting with the natural world means spending significant time in environments free of human artifice. As Breakers, we spend most of our time in constructed environments, a far cry from what we need to feed our souls. We live, travel, and work in boxes, then wonder why our souls feel boxed in.

Right at this moment, on a sunny winter day in Southern Michigan, I am looking out at Seasons, the Fetzer Institute's retreat center. Beyond, I see snow-covered hills and trees stripped bare of their summer leaves. Last night, as I walked under a near-full moon, animal sounds could be heard in the distance. Such experiences of the wildness of place put me in touch with parts of my being that get ignored in the busy-ness of the urban environment.

Practical Steps to Connect with Place

What can you do to connect your life to place? Here are a few suggestions:

- *Know your place.* Make a conscious decision to connect with your local ecology. Get to know the place and allow the place to know you. It will take ten, twenty, thirty years of constant contact. Get busy!

- *Rename yourself.* Many Keepers are known to the world by their place. For example, I have a name that I use in rituals and ceremonies. I don't declare it to the world at large, but it's something akin to "Sharif of Gaia Falls." (This place has another name, a Breaker name. It is named after the first European to find and disrupt it. Breakers name places after themselves, not the other way around.)

- *Name or rename your place.* The name of a place should reflect its dominant characteristics. Breakers often give places names that are divorced from reality. One developer in North Carolina named his residential development "Quail Hollow" though it never had quail and was a hill, not a hollow. Other developers name their subdivisions for the oaks or firs they destroyed to build their projects.

- *Regularly visit a place that is free of human artifice.* Learn how sacred it is to be in the presence of wildness. A part of my garden is staked off as wild space. Humans are not permitted to enter it or do anything to it. I will bear witness as natural forces shape that space.

- *Know where you'll go when you die.* Quite a few Menders have very specific plans for the recycling of their bodies, often involving burial in a place that is significant to them. (Breaker culture, of course, does not permit this.) How quickly do you want your body to recycle back into the Earth?

- *Leave the city.* The modern city is the epitome of Breaker thought—a human artifact that literally swallows up and kills its surroundings. We have names for air and water pollution; land pollution is called a city. The Breaker city is a machine. What would happen to you if this machine broke down for even a few days? If you live in the city now, consider whether you have alternatives. If you don't, at least decide where in nature you will go when the Breaker machine implodes. Your life may depend on it.

Reconnecting with Time

Create a Mender view of time. We must work, simultaneously, as though we can change The Mess tomorrow *and* as though we've got forever. We have to dispel the illusion that we do not have the time to make the connections.

On Overwork. Thomas Merton said that overwork is the most insidious form of violence that the nonviolent activist practices.

> There is a pervasive form of contemporary violence to which the idealist fighting for peace by non-violent methods most easily succumbs: activism and over-work. The rush and pressure of modern life are a form, perhaps the most common form, of its innate violence. To allow oneself to be carried away by a multitude of conflicting concerns, to surrender to too many demands, to commit to too many projects, to want to help everyone in everything is to succumb to violence. The frenzy of the activist neutralizes work for peace. It destroys the fruitfulness of work, because it kills the root of inner wisdom which makes work fruitful.[42]

When I consciously remove myself from Breakers' Cartesian notions of time, I realize that time can be either elastic or mechanistic. I stop overworking, reduce my stress levels, and allow time for wisdom to surface. Wisdom becomes accessible when I stand in a completely different relationship to time than the one demanded by Breakers. So, you want to change the world? Become authentic in your relationship to time.

When you consciously alter your relationship to time, everyone around you notices. Those who feel that they are trapped by time will find in your example the courage to examine their own lives.

It is important not to make this change in a quirky or weird way. Create an example that someone would want to emulate, not shun. The model you provide must be more attractive to people than the one they are currently following.

What do you believe would happen if you slowed down your life? Do you have mental tapes running that say you would fail in some way if you did not achieve certain things within a specific time frame? Who created your "normal" time frame? What would happen if you changed it? Is it possible that those mental tapes are carrying false propaganda?

It is ironic that, as I work on this section of the book, I am very conscious of my "deadline" (what a word!). All of my other work is piling up around me, meaning I "have to" work twice as hard and twice as fast to get everything done "on time." Okay, Sharif, get a grip!

Time, Entrainment, and Entrapment. Even the term "slowing down" is relativistic: it implies that the Breaker pace of thinking and acting is normal, and the way of living of our Keeper mothers and fathers is slow. The alternative way of looking at this is that Keepers' use of time is normal, and we of the Breaker society are hyperaccelerated.

One of the things that is hard-wired into our bodies is a phenomenon called *entrainment.* Simply put, the cells in our bodies try to synchronize with the rhythms of the environment. If you took a cell from my heart and a cell from your heart and put them in separate dishes, they would beat independently. But if you placed them side by side in the same dish, they would synchronize their beats. Pretty cool, yes? We learned how to do this millions of years ago.

The first and most prevalent rhythm you entrained to was the roughly one beat per second of your mother's heart. Some modern mothers play Mozart for their babies *in utero,* but their own heartbeats are far more important.

Keepers know about entrainment. The reason the drum is an almost universal element in the human world is that Keepers use it to synchronize the disparate energies in a village. Listen to how they do this. Most Keeper ceremonies drum at the same rate as the heartbeat of a healthy person at rest. War drums are at a rate similar to a person's heartbeat in an alert state.

Right now, for Breakers, the most prevalent "beat" in the world is the sixty-cycle-per-second hum of an electromagnetic motor. Right now, I can hear the whine of three different electric motors: refrigerator, fish tank, and the fan of my laptop computer. The hum is so omnipresent, we do not register it consciously. But our bodies are registering it. *They are trying to entrain to the sixty-cycle-per-second beat—at our common peril.*

What happens when the cells of your body lose the rhythm of the Earth and try to entrain to an artificial, antiorganic beat? Cancer is only one of the many manifestations of a world trying to go too fast. We fail at this hummingbirdlike pace. What happens to our health and to our psyche when we are constantly embodying failure?

It is interesting that astronauts report nausea and vomiting at levels well beyond what would be considered normal for motion sickness. As they float hundreds of miles above the Earth, they are not only completely cut off from the beat of our planet but totally surrounded by the beat of the Breakers. No wonder they want to throw up.

Thinking Past Our Lives. Another Breaker distortion of time is to use the individual lifespan as the measuring stick of all things. Nearly all our undertakings are scheduled to be accomplished and completed in a single lifetime. Keepers have no such view of time.

The lifetime of one individual is not the span in which we will be able to heal and balance the excesses of the Breaker story. Menders have long-term problems to heal, some of which may not fully manifest for a thousand years or more. These problems include

- Nuclear and chemical waste containment and disposal
- Ecological restoration and balance
- Population curbing and balance
- Transition from a cancerous growth society to a sustainable society

In order to achieve this balance and healing, Menders need to learn to think in geologic time, where five hundred years is just the blink of an eye. We need to understand and commit to projects that will take five hundred, five thousand, fifty thousand years, or more to complete.

Do you think the notion of a fifty-thousand-year project is far-fetched? Consider this: plutonium, the single most deadly substance on Earth, has a half-life of one hundred thousand years (in other words, after one hundred millennia, plutonium will still be the deadliest substance on Earth, and will have lost only half of its potency). Plutonium will still be deadly in a quarter-million years. What is the Breaker strategy for dealing with this problem of Breaker creation? Essentially none. The Hanford Nuclear Reserve has been unable to contain nuclear waste for fifty years, let alone fifty thousand.

On an admittedly different scale, there are examples of thinking that extends beyond an individual lifetime:

> [L]et us learn from those who plant dates. A date tree takes eighty years from the time it is planted to bear its first fruit. To plant a date tree is an act of faith, a sign of hope, and a symbol of one's loving commitment to the future.
>
> —MICHAEL DOWD[43]

> Let us plant dates, even though we who plant them will never eat them. . . . We must live by the love of what we will never see. This is the secret discipline. It is the refusal to let our creative act be dissolved away in immediate sense experience, and is a stubborn commitment to the future of our grandchildren. Such disciplined love is what has given prophets, revolutionaries and saints the courage to die for the future they envisaged. They make their own bodies the seed of their highest hopes.
>
> —RUBEM ALVES[44]

Or consider the master Japanese cabinet makers, who submerge their cabinets in vats of tung oil for one hundred years. When they need money, they pull out a cabinet that was placed in a vat by their great-grandfather one hundred years prior. These master carpenters are clear that they are making their cabinets for their great-grandchildren, not for themselves or their customers.

Or consider the cathedrals in Europe that took hundreds of years to build. While in the Czech Republic, I took part in a multireligious ceremony in St. Vitus Cathedral, which forms the heart of Prague Castle, the Hrad. The cathedral took 585 years to complete. Let me try to relate the significance of such a number:

> Many centuries ago, an architect comes to the people of Heidelberg, rolls out his drawings, and says: "Good people, you asked me to design for you a grand cathedral. Here it is!"
>
> As the townspeople gather around the table, the architect starts to describe the structure. "Here's the foundation. It will take one hundred years to properly finish the foundation." Some of the townspeople start counting on their fingers. "That's our lives, plus our children, plus our grandchildren."
>
> The architect then points to a different section, "These are the walls. They're fairly easy. I guess it will take about fifty years to finish the walls." By now, the townspeople had left the calculations to Emma, one of the few citizens who could count above ten without having to take off her shoes. Emma says, "It will take all the lives of our great-grandchildren to finish those walls."
>
> The architect looks a little uneasy. "Then there is the roof. That's a real problem. I think it will take 250 to 350 years to finish the roof." After a few minutes, Emma announces, "We can finish the new cathedral in the lives of our great-great-great-great-great-great-great-great-grandchildren."
>
> There is stunned silence in the room. Finally, someone at the back of the room raises his hand and says, "When do we start?"

That cathedral stands today as a testament to the townspeople's faith in the future. They had faith that there would *be* a future; that their descendants would be interested in finishing a task begun by an earlier generation; that they could transcend selfishness to dedicate their lives to a project they could never see finished. The middle seven or eight generations had to have the most faith; they would work on a project they did not start and could not finish.

These exceptions to Breaker short-term thinking demonstrate that, with sufficient motivation, we are capable of long-term thinking. Whether it is a better, more secure future for our children, or a response to a call of the Spirit, we can do what is necessary to create a world that works for all, including all future generations.

Reconnecting with the Transpersonal
We are hungry for experiences beyond our skin-encased notions of "self," where we forget our individual identities. For a brief moment, we break the boundaries that separate us from each other. Experiencing the transpersonal means losing the mental construct that this being wrapped in this skin is somehow separate and different from that being wrapped in that skin. In such moments, we have our deepest sense of being alive. This is the experience that lies at the heart of all spiritual practices. This is the essence of inclusivity.

For Keepers, a relationship to the transcendent is the norm. What non-Keepers (Breakers and Menders) call "I" is not a part of the Keeper experience. Transcendent connection to all beings, human and more-than-human, corporeal and noncorporeal, is the basis of Keeper existence.

For the rest of us, transpersonal experiences may come at moments of deep pain or pleasure. They come at moments when our attention is focused collectively on an event outside our individual selves. In Breaker society, disco dancing and watching team sports may come closest to the transpersonal experience.

Breakers don't know how to create spiritual transcendence in a disenchanted, secular society. Because of this, much Breaker transpersonal experience involves mob hysteria, manifestations of the collective shadow, and mindless chauvinism—for example, racist lynchings in the South and the Nuremberg rallies in Nazi Germany.

True transcendence is what I earlier referred to, using Christopher Alexander's term, as "the quality without a name." Once we taste it, the search for this quality becomes a central focus in our lives and the criterion by which all other experience is measured.

For Menders, the transcendent is known when we consciously connect with and choose to see that which is beyond our physical sight. Through prayer, meditation, and service to the world, we connect with others and with the Unity that contains us all.

We need something to believe in. We need something larger than our physical lives.

Connection with the Mystery

> *The most beautiful thing we can experience is the mysterious.*
> *It is the source of all true art and science.*
>
> —ALBERT EINSTEIN[45]

The Web of Life consists of the self-regulating, self-evolving interactions of countless billions of beings. For more than a million years, humans have existed within the Web of Life, within the Earth's regenerative processes, in balance with all other beings.[46]

There is a Spirit that permeates, forms, and regulates the Web of Life and all parts of its "body," including the human family. This Spirit doesn't belong to anyone. It isn't "my Spirit" or "my Love," or even "my Mind." This is as absurd as saying "my Columbia River." I may drink from the river, swim in it, even urinate in it, but the river isn't mine. One's experience of the Spirit can be personalized, but that experience is not the reality. The more we experience the Web, the more we experience the Spirit. The multiplicity and diversity of our connections with other beings reinforces our connection with the Spirit.

Reconnecting with the Spirit involves facing fear so that it no longer maintains its grip on our life. Keepers and Menders, human beings who live within the sacred, are not motivated by fear and lack. It's not that they are superhumans who are impervious to pain. They do feel pain, but don't *fear* it.

Absence of fear does not imply a refusal to recognize real threats to one's life, liberty, or well-being. It means that fear is no longer the primary motivating factor in one's life. For example, I have been afraid of dogs. That fear used to paralyze me. I could not even pet a happy, nonthreatening dog. Now, though I am no longer ruled by dog fear, I will still avoid a growling, barking, unchained dog. Not being motivated by fear does not mean taking leave of common sense.

A person who is not locked in personal fear can be open to an encounter with the spiritual. Mystical experience—that is, direct experience of the Spirit—lies beyond the limits of language and mental perception.

> I was participating in a workshop held on the beautiful Santiam River, which winds through the Cascade mountains of Oregon. Across from the rustic lodge was a waterfall tumbling into the crystal-clear, ice-cold river waters. Cliffs rose on all sides, making a dramatic scene.
>
> Up river a few hundred yards, a yellow bus disgorged its passengers onto a small beach that was the tip of a state park. The passengers, mainly black and Hispanic and almost all teenagers, were inmates at MacLaren Youth Correction Facility on a rare outing.
>
> During a break in my workshop, I sat outside the lodge and one of the young men came over to me with a look on

his face of wonder mixed with disbelief, and a good measure of confusion thrown in. "What do you think of all this?" I asked him as we both surveyed the panorama.

He shook his head slowly. "I don't know," he said, holding his hand to his chest. "Something's happening."

"Yes," I said to him, "something is happening." We sat a few minutes together, then I asked him, "Do you like what's happening?"

He was still trying to work through his confusion. "I think so. I was thinking that when the bus goes back, I'll try to remember which way it goes, so I can come back here when I get released." He paused again. "Something is happening here," he said, again touching his heart.

This young man was having a mystical experience—a spiritually meaningful experience that cannot be described in words. The reform school guards had no idea that this young man was in the midst of spiritual turmoil, coming face to face with beauty and the sacred but with no way of understanding and affirming the experience. Our ability to receive, understand, and translate mystical experiences is a function of how deeply embedded in the wisdom culture, the Mender culture, we are. Reform school guards are not selected on the basis of their spiritual awareness. They are selected because they are good at Breaker functions—control and domination.

Practical Steps to Connect with the Spirit
What can we do to connect our lives to the Spirit? Here are a few suggestions:

- See the sacred in your own life. See the divine aspect of "ordinary" events like riding downtown or attending a meeting.
- Adopt a regular practice of meditation, celebration, contemplation, or prayer. Try to give at least twenty minutes

per day to this. However, do not become rigid regarding the time and place of your practice. Even if you have only ninety seconds for meditation or prayer, perhaps sitting in your car before you start the engine, value that time.

- If you are already acquainted with the presence and power of the Spirit, become a support and guide to others who are sincerely seeking the same awareness.
- Share what you learn from spiritual conferences and workshops with those who cannot afford to attend.
- Be willing to truly do things in a new way. Be willing to be a Mender.

This chapter has been about sword sharpening. By practicing enoughness, committing ourselves to inclusive compassion, and making essential reconnections, we have started to develop our hearts for the arduous task of reshaping a society.

So, now that we have the tools, what do we do with them?

8

THE EXTERNAL REVOLUTION— PRACTICING INCLUSIVITY WITH OTHERS

It's not by anything we think, not by something we figure out in our heads. We're transformed by what we do.
—CHARLOTTE JOKO BECK[47]

Flying Below the Radar

MENDERS ARE ALREADY active in the world, creating the consciousness, cultures, and institutions of a new society. The actions of Menders are not generally visible to mainstream media. We are "flying below the radar" of Breaker culture. In a society obsessed with overconsumption and the lifestyles of the rich and famous, Menders are plain boring. The goal of Menders is not to appear on a talk show or to have a thirty-second sound bite on a television news program. Their goal is to transform themselves and to contribute to the transformation of their society.

Creating a Parallel Society

The Mender society will be built on the ordinary actions of ordinary people. It will consist of people eating, sleeping, working, washing clothes, finding each other, celebrating victories, and grieving together. The Mender society will *parallel* the world of the Breakers.

Not all of us are going to walk on the Moon or expand our consciousness or become one with the Divine or find true community (or even true love). And even if we do, we will still find that we have to "chop wood, carry water." Not all of us are going to commune with extraterrestrials or climb Mount Everest, but we will all, in the words of Buddhist scholar Charlotte Joko Beck, "make love, drive freeway."[48] In our focus on the peak, sublime experiences, we tend to ignore or take for granted the mundane experiences that make up most of our lives.

We go to a weekend workshop and come back announcing that the event "transformed my life." But nothing about our life changes. We continue to go to the same job, fill out the same forms in triplicate that we care nothing about, put our money in the bank, eat processed food, watch commercials. The only thing that has changed is that we now have a vivid memory of a "peak" experience.

A world that works for all is one where our mundane actions serve our deepest individual and collective needs. In such a world, the possibility of the beautiful and the sublime exists because we have taken care of the ordinary.

Revolution, Not Resistance

> *Our first task is to create a shadow economic, social and even technological structure that will be ready to take over as the existing system fails.*
>
> —DAVID EHRENFELD[49]

Menders are not a resistance movement seeking to undermine Breaker society. Our goal is to provide true alternatives, based on a fundamentally different way of thinking. In our parallel society, all of the things that humans do to support life, beauty, and creativity will be done in a sustainable, life-affirming way.

Do people use electricity in the Breaker society? Then Menders will supply electricity in a decentralized, responsible, ecologically efficient way that rewards conservation and penalizes overconsumption and waste. Are people entertained in a Breaker society? Then Menders will foster the conditions for entertainment, unleashing the creativity of the community. Do people drink water and eat food in the Breaker society? Menders will create sustainable delivery systems for our food and water, in harmony with Nature.

We do not know exactly what the Mender society will look like. I could pretend that I did and predict that all of us will be wearing Birkenstocks and flying around with jet packs in the year 2020. In reality, trying to predict what will happen next year, or even next month, is foolhardy. Our present lives could not have been predicted even fifteen years ago. One of my favorite examples of the inability to predict the future is former East German leader Erich Honecker's statement, "The Berlin Wall will stand another hundred years." Less than one hundred *hours* later, the wall was breached.

What we are creating now is the bridge to a Mender society, not the society itself.

What People Are Doing to Catalyze an Inclusive Society

There are many ways in which people are catalyzing a change in consciousness and action. It would be impossible in this space to catalogue everything that is being done, but this section hints at the breadth of the movement.

Transforming Politics: Creating the Politics of Fulfillment

> *Withdrawing in disgust is not the same thing as apathy.*
> —SLACKER *(movie)*

We can create a society that lives up to our political ideals, not down to the lowest common denominator of superficiality, mud-slinging, and name-calling. Instead of feeling powerless, hopeless, cynical, and alienated, we can find satisfaction and fulfillment in the sphere of human governance. We can create a political system in which the Golden Rule forms the basis of all domestic and foreign policy.

Ending the Politics of Fear and Hatred
At present, running for political office is simple: raise enough money to run a campaign that will instill fear of your opponent in a plurality of the electorate. This is the epitome of Breaker consciousness: "I am separate from that evil person over there. Vote for me because I am less evil than he [or she] is."

Many people are working to end this political situation by

- Refusing to vote for any candidate who employs or allows negative campaigning.
- Voting to limit all terms of office. By increasing the number of people who hold elective office and decreasing the power, prestige, and money that stem from incumbency, we can make our political system more democratic. Office holders will be seen more as representatives of the citizenry than as wielders of power. (Ernest Callenbach takes this one step further: he proposes doing away with elections altogether.[50] Representatives would be appointed at random from phone directories and automobile registration lists. The argument is that political representation should be treated much like jury duty.)
- Supporting voter initiatives that limit campaign spending, so that elections are not determined by a preponderance of funds.
- Promoting initiatives that require winning candidates to have votes from at least 50 percent of all eligible voters. If "none of the above" is the top vote-getter, the election

has to be rescheduled, with new candidates. (This practice, known as *voto en blanco,* is already in use in several Central American countries.)

- Campaigning for a Constitutional Convention. Our current Constitution, the core of which was written over two hundred years ago, does not reflect in any way the challenges, values, and realities of the society we find ourselves in now (it didn't then either). In fact, Thomas Jefferson believed that the document was not intended to last more than twenty years. The goal of a Constitutional Convention would be not so much to reform the existing Constitution as to write a new one, to develop a set of shared principles upon which the entire nation could agree, perhaps starting with a Bill of Responsibilities.

Transforming Economics: Creating a Society of Enoughness

While *you* may be living according to the principles of simplicity and abundance, there is no assurance that your neighbors are. Wasteful overconsumption anywhere destabilizes the entire system and turns up the volume on greed, envy, and feelings of scarcity and superiority.

In order to free the wealth of our communities, we have to create structural incentives for enoughness and disincentives for conspicuous overconsumption. Around the country, many grassroots organizations are advocating the following measures:

Wealth and Income Controls

Money addiction is the only form of addiction where the addicts are given near exclusive control of the object of their craving. If we are to survive, we must radically reform this scenario. Menders are trying to end the cycle of money addiction by supporting measures that will discourage the accumulation of wealth and income. These include:

- Progressive income taxes
- Luxury taxes
- Consumption taxes
- Lower taxes for those who voluntarily restrict their incomes and assets according to community-based standards of "enoughness."
- Additional incentives to those who pledge to maintain their family income at even lower "sustainability" levels. These incentives could include free "lifeline" utilities and services, like water, electricity, telephone service, basic health maintenance, and public transportation.
- Greater restraints on corporations, including
  Strict enforcement of existing antitrust laws and the addition of some new ones. (Small really is beautiful.)
  Limits on a corporation's ability to move capital, resources, and work in the quest for near-slave labor.
  "Capital punishment" for corporations found guilty of a crime that causes the death of humans. The corporation would be dissolved and its assets seized and distributed for public purposes. The shareholders would lose their investment—punishment for investing in a morally bankrupt business.
- Community wealth measurements. If bank accounts and material possessions constitute an individual's wealth, what defines a community's wealth? The most well-known Breaker standard is the Gross Domestic Product (GDP), which measures the total annual output of goods and services. The fallacy is that whatever sends GDP up is good, even a human disaster that brings business to medical and construction companies. Emerging alternatives to GDP include Portland's livability standards, the Sustainable Seattle campaign, and the "real progress indicators" favored by some other cities.

- Community banks and loan funds, barter exchange networks, locally rooted credit unions, and alternative currencies, which form the backbone of a new, sustainable, inclusive economy. Global corporatism is not the answer.

Mender Economic Development

Global development should not mean making the world safe for global corporatism. It should not mean plowing up local markets or turning artisans, farmers, and craftspeople into employees. Globalization should mean strengthening local markets and economies, tying them together into an interdependent web.

In Mender economic development, the community will be the primary building block for development—not the individual, the corporation, or the state. This approach to development calls for something beyond capitalism and communism, or any other economic theory currently in vogue. "Creating a world that works for all" must mean enhancing and improving what already works well in each locale.

Transforming the Spiritual: Creating a Society of the Spirit

Menders recognize that the sacred and the secular are not separate concepts but are interlinked and ultimately the same. We also reject the notion that enlightenment, mystical awareness, and oneness with the Divine are experiences reserved for the holy few. Jesus is said to have declared, "I and the Father are One." I do not think he was articulating a unique relationship as much as an awareness of the natural connection between humans and God. Similarly, the Buddha taught that his experience of enlightenment was potentially available to everyone.

Matthew Fox has said that the world's religions are like wells plugged into the same underground river. Our wisdom teachers have been our guides to the wells and have described their contents. Organized religion, on the other hand, has attempted to limit our experience of the wells. It has also taught us that somehow the water in "our" well is better than the water in "their" wells. Breakers who are "fundamentalist" think "my" well is the only one with water in it.

Religion as Help and Hindrance on the Path
Does your religion matter to you—other than as something to do on Sunday or as a mumbled "God Bless America" at the end of political rallies? Does your religious practice actually mean anything to you? To the world?

Your faith should be a healing force in the world. This happens when spiritual understanding is allowed to shape your behavior—rather than the other way around. When faith is deep and values are clear, your actions become both powerful and authentic. By contrast, when faith is shallow and values conflicted, actions are of little effect and religion becomes "the opium of the masses."

If my everyday actions are not consistent with the central premises of my faith, my professing a religion is not only meaningless but misleading. To say "I'm a Christian" yet act in a way that would make Jesus puke only serves to discredit Christianity as a potentially effective force for change in the world. The same is true with every other spiritual teaching. What we do speaks louder than what we say.

> *We walk, and our religion is shown (even to the dullest and most insensitive person) in how we walk. Or to put it more accurately, living in this world means choosing, choosing to walk, and the way we choose to walk is infallibly and perfectly expressed in the walk itself. Nothing can disguise it. The walk of an ordinary man and of an enlightened man are as different as that of a snake and a giraffe.*
>
> —R. H. BLYTH[51]

So, what is your real religion?

The Breaker religion professes a belief in a god who has no real power and doesn't particularly give a hoot about anything important. A god who seems to be very concerned about whether boys are having sex with other boys but doesn't much care about the destruction of tens of thousands of species, the pollution of an entire global ecological system, or whether children around the world are starving to death. A god who apparently has less power than the Breakers themselves have. This is an impotent, "I am separate" god, born of the limited Breaker consciousness.

If our faith is not a healing force in the world, it doesn't really matter whether or not we even have a faith. A Christian who doesn't practice the Golden Rule is exactly the same as an atheist who doesn't practice the Golden Rule.

From a correspondence between beliefs and actions, we can begin to create a Society of the Spirit.

Evidence that such a society is in the making is plentiful:

- People are recognizing that an inclusive spiritual society is polyreligious—highly tolerant of diverse religious expressions. It doesn't matter if people believe a certain way, have multiple and conflicting beliefs, or have no transcendental beliefs at all. It also doesn't matter if people make up new religious expressions. Inclusivity recognizes that there simply is no one right way to do things.

- Allegiance doesn't matter. Breaker society says a person is Christian *or* Buddhist *or* Muslim *or* . . . Menders, on the other hand, recognize that people may be Christian *and* Buddhist *and* Muslim *and* . . . Many today are following several religious traditions, believing that the apparent contradictions are unimportant.

Not Christian or Jew or Muslim, not Hindu,
Buddhist, sufi, or zen. Not any religion

or cultural system. I am not from the East
or the West, not out of the ocean or up

from the ground, not natural or ethereal, not
composed of elements at all. I do not exist,

am not an entity in this world or the next,
did not descend from Adam and Eve or any

origin story. My place is placeless, a trace
of the traceless. Neither body or soul.

I belong to the beloved, have seen the two
worlds as one and that one call to and know,

first, last, outer, inner, only that
breath breathing human being.

—JELALUDDIN RUMI[52]

Developing Community Transcendence
Menders are creating ceremonies and rituals that root the community's common transcendent experience. Whether in an opening or closing ceremony for meetings or in a group-honoring exercise for community meals, Menders are finding opportunities to focus a group's thoughts outside the individual and toward the transcendent.

Developing a Real Spiritual Dialogue
Spirituality, to be a healing force in the world, must move from a discussion of how many angels can dance on the head of a pin to, say, how we can develop a new apartment project from a spiritual perspective. Menders are recognizing that common ground is to be found in an exercise of the spirit.

Seeing the Spirit of The Other

One way to develop the spiritual conversation is to participate in the rituals and traditions of The Other. For example, some Catholics are participating in Jewish and Islamic religious services. Also, people of different faiths are coming together in ecumenical activities and conferences. They do so with the intent not to convert but to broaden their understanding.

The Longer Struggle: Creating a Soul-Filled Society

Renouncing the Mall

About 2,500 years ago, before there was the Buddha, there was young Prince Gautama. His father gave him a life of sublime comfort and ease. All the pleasures of the kingdom were showered on the young prince.

Gautama's father went even further. He removed all traces of pain and suffering—including old age, illness, and death—from his son's sight. Unfortunately for the father, and to the great fortune of the world, he was unsuccessful: Prince Gautama came to experience all forms of suffering and transcended them, becoming the Buddha, the Enlightened One.

But what if his father had succeeded? What if he had constructed a world for his son where there simply was no suffering? What if young Gautama had never left the palace where only good things happened and where he was shielded from all negativity? And what if that shield had been extended to cover a whole society? What would that society have looked like?

It would probably have looked a lot like the regional mall.

The people, young and old, who are rejecting the "mall" life are seeking the same thing that Gautama sought: a life where deep joy and deep pain can be reconciled within the human heart; a place where life takes on a larger significance. In a multireligious ceremony I attended at Prague Castle, the Roman Catholic Archbishop of Prague said, "It is the purpose of religion to make us feel pain, to connect us with the suffering of the world." Unless you can feel both joy and pain, your heart is undeveloped.

Our children want meaning and connection. What they get is the mall, a place where all conditions are rigidly controlled for maximum comfort. It is always 70 degrees, rain and snow are unknown, and never is heard a discouraging word (or if it is, wired and uniformed security guards will quickly silence it). This world from which struggle and difficulty have been banished supports our lies and denials, removes us from personal responsibility (and therefore personal power), and plunges us into a passivity that makes our hearts grow soft and weak from disuse. In this world, we no longer know how to grieve, because grief has been rendered superfluous.

The opposite of the mall also exists. It's called Camden, New Jersey. The suffering that is denied in the mall simply piles up in Camden, and in the other waste-heaps of human misery found in urban areas around the world. Constant suffering without meaning, constant pain without context, are as inhuman and debilitating as no suffering at all.

I hope and pray and work for a Mender world that will be neither Camden nor the mall. I envision a world where our children have hearts that have been opened by experiences both of suffering and of joy—experiences through which they have been guided by loving peers, adults, and elders.

Like joy and peace, tears, pain, and suffering are parts of the ensouling process. Without them, we inwardly wither and die.

The Commons: An Answer to the Mall

What would a society of inclusivity look like? How would it function? Most important, how can we create the conditions for this society to develop?

What is the center of your community? Years ago, it was the local market or the local church. Now, there simply is no center. Without a center, we drift, looking for direction and finding none. We latch on to the latest superficial fad, or we search the skies for beings from other planets who might give us answers.

There is an alternative to this. We can choose to combine our strength, our resources, and our spirit in an effort to create a new center for a new society. We can recreate the Commons. The Commons can be a primary engine for the spread and development of Mender consciousness.

Historically, every society has had a public common space at its heart. The common area served as the social gathering spot, marketplace, a stage for public events (from legal pronouncements to lynchings), and the financial heart of the community. America's most famous commons, Boston Common, was the place where people grazed their sheep. In early America, the public squares and public houses were the places to discuss and debate our political future.

The Commons is the place to experiment and to practice the values of a new society. The key value of the mall is profit. The key value of the Commons is inclusivity. The Commons is where people connect with each other. The Commons is the resurrection of the local market, the local polis, the spiritual center of local society.

A VISION OF THE COMMONS

I walk into the Commons, not really having a destination. The Commons is where my basic community needs are satisfied: to see and be seen, to connect with others, to know that we are part of the same community.

There are plenty of excuses to be in the Commons, from the coffee to the books to the movies. I may bring my knives to be sharpened, my laundry to be cleaned, my muscles to be exercised, my brain to be stimulated, my heart to be uplifted.

I may have come to attend a meeting, spend time at the crafts center, work in one of the many microenterprises, or just hang out.

My first stop is certain: the Commons Bank, to exchange dollars for Commons Credits. While most of the enterprises in the Commons take dollars, things are much cheaper when I use Commons Credits. And every time I exchange and use Commons Credits, I get points toward my ownership in the Commons.

That's one of the main things everyone likes about the Commons that we don't like about the mall: *we own it*. Every time we buy something, every time a merchant pays rent, every time a community group uses the meeting spaces, we earn ownership credits. At my current rate, in two or three years, I will own enough points to start receiving dividend checks. If I work hard enough and spend my money and my time at the Commons, I will increase my ownership—a form of social security. If I take care of the Commons, the Commons will take care of me. (No matter how much money I spend at McDonalds, I will never own it.) And according to the Commons Plan, within five years, our community will own the majority of the stock!

That's not to say that this place doesn't have its share of problems. When the tattoo parlor moved in, a large segment of the Commons community threatened to leave. There were even several days of picketing, which of course attracted a lot of media attention. Management used it as a way of showing how we resolve our problems by dialogue and consensus.

The Commons is the place where our community develops itself. The Commons is the means by which capital (physical, economic, social, and spiritual) is fed into the community. We don't exactly know where we are going, but we know that the Commons will help us get there.

The Commons as Community

The Commons is like an urban monastery, a shelter in the midst of a decaying civilization. In the busyness and madness of Breaker society, the Commons is a place where everyone comes together to slow down, to pause, to contemplate. It is the place to have a cup of coffee or a glass of beer and a conversation with others. It is the common ground that has been usurped by the mall and the television.

Among the things that the Commons provides are

- A domain of safety and mutual respect where community members can engage each other on equal terms.
- Activities expressly designed to support ethnic, ideological, and class diversity.
- A broad range of opportunities for "right livelihood" and "right relationships."
- Creative outlets of all kinds.
- A performance space that can also be used for community meetings and services.

The Economic Commons

- The Commons is a marketplace for locally grown, produced, and crafted goods and services.
- The Commons stimulates the vitality of its own local economy while also promoting connections with other local economies around the globe.
- The Commons is the base for a local sustainable currency, a medium of exchange not subject to the whims of global corporate forces but based on the trust, faith, and resources of the locality.
- The Commons supports basic economic community activities, including the provision of food, housing, energy, transportation, health care services, and entertainment.

- Local ownership and control are hard-wired into the Commons; outside ownership is disfavored. The Commons has five equal classes of stock: investor, employee, consumer, neighborhood (for people who live near the Commons), and environmental (held in trust for nonhuman beings). In this way, the Commons can be fully responsive to its total community.
- Profits from the Commons have one function: to make the local community stronger.

The Ecology Commons

A cleaner world and respectful and saner uses of natural resources are rising on the global agenda as we enter the twenty-first century. The Commons addresses the movement to save the planet in a number of ways.

The Commons includes a major regional learning and teaching center on ecology. In collaboration with the region's public school systems, the Commons provides coordinated, in-depth courses on all aspects of the environment. In addition to public school tours, the Commons sponsors youth-oriented projects and activities, especially for the inner city youth who reside in the surrounding area.

As part of its educational function, the Commons serves as a showroom of state-of-the-art appropriate technology. From energy generation to waste recovery, the Ecology Commons is a walk-through laboratory of methods that can be implemented right now to preserve our ecology. The Ecology Commons also provides office and meeting space for environmental organizations, local, regional, and national. The Ecology Commons is a central clearing house for these organizations.

The Spiritual Commons

The Spiritual Commons brings people together for the exploration and service of the Spirit.

It is easy to say what the Spiritual Commons is not. It's not a church, masjid, temple, or synagogue, though it has aspects of each. It is not a place for the teaching of Christianity, Islam, Buddhism, Santeria, Zen, or any other specific spiritual philosophy, though all of the above may be practiced there. What the Spiritual Commons is can be understood in terms of a few essential characteristics:

- The Spiritual Commons is the place where the inclusive aspects of all religions are practiced. Diverse spiritual rituals, including new and unconventional ones, are performed there every day.
- All participating groups open their practices to everyone, but beyond providing information when it is requested, they don't engage in evangelizing or conversion efforts on the premises.
- Each group is committed to participating in at least one other group's practices.
- A range of secondary activities, including discussion groups and social events, cater to the spiritual needs of everyone in the community, whether or not they participate in formal rituals.

By renouncing the mall, by re-creating the Commons, we can develop the conditions that will lead us to a truly soul-filled society.

CONCLUSION

MAKING THE COMMITMENT

YOU HAVE COME to the end of this book. You have read about our societal problems, collectively dubbed The Mess. You have read about what holds us back from effective action for a new society. You have read about the spirit, consciousness, values, and actions it will take to make a world that works for all. You have read about what that world could look like.

Now, what are you going to do?

If you are like me, you get stirred up by something that you have read or heard, decide you want to take action, then get bogged down by the immensity and logistics of the task. You may fall prey to procrastination: "Maybe I can get started next week." Or you may find that your Breaker lifestyle simply does not support your desire for change.

You are not alone. But somehow you must rally your will to overcome these apparent obstacles. Now is the time to make a commitment. Now is the time to make your life matter. Now is the time to take the Mender Pledge.

What Is a Pledge? Where Is Your Allegiance?

Remember, years ago, standing beside your school desk, hand over your heart, reciting the Pledge of Allegiance in unison with your fellow students?

I pledge allegiance	(What the heck does that mean?)
to the flag	(I know that one: the cloth on a stick in the corner.)
of the United States of America	(That's the funny-shaped, multi-colored blob on a map in another corner. I have to memorize the state capitals.)
and to the republic for which it stands	(Huh?)
one nation, under God	(God's the guy with the long beard they talk about in church on Sunday.)
indivisible	(I wonder, is that like "invisible"?)
with liberty and justice for all.	(Huh?)

This unvarying and largely meaningless exercise was drilled into us at an early age. Its repetition did not increase its meaning for us—in fact, probably the opposite was true. The Pledge of Allegiance was just a routine to get through in the morning.

Most of us do not attach a rich set of meanings to United States citizenship. We don't have a clear understanding of the distinction between citizenship and the accident of birth in a particular spot, of particular parents. Aside from the mumbled Pledge of Allegiance, we Americans do not have a common bond, and it shows. It is ironic that our most knowledgeable and sincerely patriotic Americans are newly naturalized immigrants. They are the ones who have actually given up something—their old citizenship—in order to take the pledge. They are the ones who have studied the Constitution, the Declaration of Independence, the Bill of Rights. They have had their personal lives scrutinized. They have passed the tests. They truly know what it means to be American.

Some of us faced other pledges in our lives—as Boy Scouts, as Army inductees, as politicians. If you are in a relationship, you may have made a pledge of commitment to your partner. Decades ago, as a new inductee to the Federal bar in North Carolina, I made a pledge to uphold the Constitution of the United States against all enemies, foreign and domestic. (For me, at the time, this meant defending the Constitution from Senator Jesse Helms.)

What do these pledges mean? What do they ask us to do? What do they ask us to sacrifice? What responsibilities and rights are embodied in the pledges? The unfortunate reality is that very little is asked and very little is offered.

Our challenge is to make a commitment that is big enough to really stir us.

During the height of the Vietnam War, as I turned eighteen and became eligible for the draft, I realized that I could not go to Vietnam to kill people just because the U.S. government thought that was a good idea. I also realized that "Conscientious Objector" status was unavailable, because (at the time) I could not honestly declare that I did not believe in taking a life.

My realization was more than a personal decision about whether or not to fight. I deeply believed that the government did not have the right to compel me to participate in murder. Although family and friends counseled me to register, get my draft card, and "see what happens," I believed that any level of participation in an evil system was itself evil.

I made a commitment to not participate in the draft system—essentially, a commitment to do nothing. My choice could have cost me five years in Leavenworth Prison. I did not want to go to prison. But I also knew that I could not comply with the draft law.

> Through the Grace of the Divine, I did not go to prison and I did not go to war. Since that time, I have made other commitments, but none as grave and powerful as my decision to do nothing during the Vietnam War.

Right now, you are being asked to make a commitment, to stand up for something. You do not have to put your life at risk, as the signers of the Declaration of Independence did, nor do you necessarily have to do anything as difficult as going to prison or facing down skinheads. Only you know what and how much you are willing to sacrifice. In our present times, it is significant if you are willing to pledge your soft, comfortable lifestyle.

In his farewell address as Oregon governor, Neil Goldschmidt challenged his listeners to "name one hard thing your government asks you to do." His question was rhetorical: everyone knew they couldn't come up with an answer. If we are going to create a Mender society, we have to reject the pampered existence of the mall. We have to find that "one hard thing" to do. It may be work that is unpleasant and unpopular. But we will find that there are many, many others working beside us.

I believe there are literally tens of millions of Menders out there. One of the reasons we do not recognize each other is that there is no common language, common symbology, common culture that unites us. The Mender Pledge is designed to change that.

The Mender Pledge is designed to help us clarify our commitment, identify ourselves to each other, and mobilize enough people to catalyze a profound transformation of our society.

Identifying Menders

Many of us feel isolated, and therefore powerless, right in the midst of the multitude. Right now, as I'm writing these words in one of my favorite coffeehouses, there is a young man sitting at the next table, a stack of papers in front of him, an iced latte in his hand, deeply intent on his writing. What are his beliefs? There is nothing in his demeanor, his looks, or what he's writing that can tell me whether or not he is a Mender. But I wish I knew, for then a valuable dialogue might be possible. If we are to rid ourselves of our hopelessness, we have to find ways to identify ourselves to each other as Menders.

Years ago, there was a powerful organization called Beyond War whose goal was to eliminate armed conflict on this planet. People who took the Beyond War pledge would wear a small Earth pin as a sign of their commitment.

The pin acted as a nonverbal code: those who did not know about Beyond War saw only an attractive personal ornament; those who had come into contact with the movement saw a person with whom they shared a fundamental commitment to a better world.

Menders could adopt a similar device. Anyone who has taken the Mender Pledge could wear a simple button, conveying to like-minded people that he or she has made a commitment to fundamental consciousness change.

Catalyzing Transformation

While both statistics and intuition indicate that most of us want the Mender shift to an inclusive society, a movement has not yet coalesced. Many people quote anthropologist Margaret Mead, who observed how a small group of committed people could change the world. How small? How committed?

In innovation diffusion theory,[53] researchers have discovered that a change becomes inevitable when 5 to 15 percent of a population accepts the change. These "early adopters" catalyze the change for others; they make the innovation understandable, acceptable, "normal."

This means that Menders will need to mobilize around 26 million people in the United States. The primary vehicle for mobilization will be the Mender Pledge. Getting such a vast number to

THE MENDER PLEDGE

I believe in inclusivity. I believe that our lives are inextricably linked one to another. We cannot wage war against anyone without waging war against ourselves. Therefore, I will practice inclusivity with myself, my family, my community, the natural world, and all others. I will actively work toward the goal of an inclusive society, a world that works for all.

I know that we are One. Therefore, I will give to you what I want for me. I know there is enough for all.

I want everyone to win. Therefore, I will work to resolve all conflicts to every party's satisfaction.

I want acceptance. Therefore, I will accept myself for who and what I am, I will accept you for who and what you are, and I will accept all others for who and what they are. Even if I resist your behavior, I will accept you as a Child of God, a part of the Divine.

I want no harm. Therefore, I will not harm myself or you or any others, by thought, word, or deed.

I want forgiveness. Therefore, I will forgive myself, I will forgive you, and I will forgive all others.

I want to be free. Therefore, I will not let others dominate, control, or manipulate me. And I will not dominate, control, or manipulate you or others.

I want peace. Therefore, I will be peaceful with myself, with you, and with others.

I want love. Therefore, I will love myself, I will love you, and I will love all others.

As outward expressions of my commitment, I will

- Register my pledge
- Invite others to make similar pledges
- Wear an inclusivity button
- Regularly attend at least one Mender meeting in my area and offer to host it periodically
- Organize a local Mender meeting if none already exists
- Hold inclusivity workshops and trainings
- Commit at least 10 percent of my time, money, and/or resources to the creation of an inclusive society

I find it hard to do the right thing when people react to me out of fear or lack. At those times, I want to separate from them, see them as wrong or evil or just different. I want to defend myself. Then I realize that all of the discord, disharmony, and disease in the world comes from the futile attempt to defend against that which is within us. I will create bridges across our fears, our pain, and our illusion of lack. It may take several attempts, but I will succeed. And we all shall win.

pledge to inclusivity will not be easy. However, to paraphrase Lao Tzu, a movement of 26 million signatures begins with a single pledge: mine.

It doesn't matter how long it takes to collect the necessary pledges. It could take anywhere from five months to five years. Nor should we keep obsessive tallies of media coverage, web site hits, elections won, money gathered, or any of the other statistics dear to Breaker hearts. Our success is measured by internal standards: Did I practice inclusivity today? More than yesterday? Did I encourage others to do so? Am I living up to my pledge?

Action, Commitment, and Consequences

Most people know the first few lines of the Declaration of Independence. Few know the last sentence. However, it was the last sentence that was the most consequential for the signers:

> *And for the support of this Declaration, with a firm reliance on the protection of Divine Providence, we mutually pledge to each other our Lives, our Fortunes and our sacred Honor.*

They realized that they were not just signing a statement of principles; they were signing their own death warrants. They all knew the penalty for defying the king. What we now call patriotism was known by another name to the British Crown—sedition. King George had powerful tools at his disposal with which to punish offensive activity. The signers of the Declaration of Independence would not merely have sacrificed their lives. After the king had had them drawn and quartered, and their heads boiled in oil, he would have seized all their property, turning their wives and children out into the streets to become beggars. Finally, the Crown would have seized their names: their children could no longer have called themselves Jefferson or Hamilton or Adams. All reference to the seditious persons would have been expunged from the records.

They would have ceased to exist. Signing the Declaration of Independence made their commitment to each other and to a new society irrevocable.

In more recent times, Václav Havel and the other signers of Charter 77 in Czechoslovakia knew that by speaking out they would face immediate and harsh reprisals at the hands of the Soviet-backed government. As of this writing, Nobel laureate Aung San Suu Kyi of Myanmar still suffers at the hands of that country's military dictatorship solely because she has pledged herself to the path of democracy and human freedom.

Right now, I am asking you to make a commitment, a pledge to inclusivity. The consequences of your pledge will by no means be as dramatic or as dangerous as the ones taken by Jefferson, Havel, or Suu Kyi. You won't be threatened with death or imprisonment. You won't be forced to do anything. The thing that will be threatened by your taking the Mender pledge is your Breaker consciousness, your Breaker behavior, your overly consumptive and soul-emptying lifestyle.

Make the commitment, then act. Action makes the pledge "real," visible to yourself and others.

Once you have made the pledge to an inclusive society, once you have committed to act, you will know the right thing to do. In fact, it doesn't matter what you do—your pledge will focus your action. Release the notion of results, act in the purity of your Spirit. Like me, you may focus your action on telling others about the revolution to a society based on inclusivity. Or your Mender Pledge may inspire you to start an inclusivity reading circle, build the Commons, develop an alternative school, organize a food cooperative, introduce yourself to your neighbors, mobilize your community, start a political movement, investigate a decentralized utility system, generate your own electricity, create an alternative currency, or do any of scores of other Mender activities.

So, once you put this book down, what are you going to do?

NOTES

1. This essay originally appeared in *Civilization,* April/May 1998. It is used with permission of the author.
2. Coleman Barks, *The Essential Rumi* (San Francisco: HarperSanFrancisco, 1995), 16.
3. Michael Dowd, *Earthspirit* (Mystic, Conn.: Twenty-Third Publications, 1992), 81.
4. Eknath Easwaran, *The Compassionate Universe* (Petaluma, Calif.: Nilgiri Press, 1989), 22.
5. Authors Calvin Luther Martin and David Abram use the term "more than human" to describe what we usually refer to as the "natural" world, a term that implies that there is an "unnatural" or "better than natural" world. David Abram, *The Spell of the Sensuous* (New York: Vintage, 1996); Calvin Luther Martin, *In the Spirit of the Earth* (Baltimore: Johns Hopkins University Press, 1992).
6. Daniel Schorr, "The World's Whimsical Spending Habits," *Christian Science Monitor,* 20 September 1996, 18.
7. Lester Brown et al., *State of the World 1998: A Worldwatch Institute Report on Progress Toward a Sustainable Society* (New York: W. W. Norton, 1998), 22.
8. *New York Times Magazine,* August 1964.

9. Christopher Alexander, *The Timeless Way of Building* (New York: Oxford University Press, 1979), ix.

10. Sharif Abdullah, *The Power of One: Authentic Leadership in Turbulent Times,* 3rd ed. (Gabriola Island, B.C.: New Society Publishers, 1995).

11. Vimala Thakar, *The Eloquence of Living: Meeting Life with Freshness, Fearlessness, and Compassion* (San Rafael, Calif.: New World Library, 1989), 53.

12. Daniel Quinn, *Ishmael* (New York: Bantam, 1993), 11.

13. Ray Marshall, "The Global Jobs Crisis," *Foreign Policy,* fall 1995, 50.

14. Václav Havel, "The Power of the Powerless," in *The Power of the Powerless,* ed. Steven Lukes (Armonk, N.Y.: M. E. Sharpe, 1985), 27.

15. Sogyal Rinpoche, *The Tibetan Book of Living and Dying* (San Francisco: HarperSanFrancisco, 1992), 174–180.

16. Cheri Huber, *That Which You Are Seeking Is Causing You to Seek* (Mountain View, Calif.: Center for the Practice of Zen Buddhist Meditation, 1990), 17.

17. Barbara Marx Hubbard, *Conscious Evolution: Awakening the Power of Our Social Potential* (Novato, Calif.: New World Library, 1998).

18. David Korten, *When Corporations Rule the World* (San Francisco: Berrett-Koehler, 1995); *The Post-Corporate World* (San Francisco: Berrett-Koehler, 1999).

19. Ken Wilber, *Sex, Ecology, Spirituality: The Spirit of Evolution* (Boston: Shambhala, 1995).

20. Lester Milbrath, *Envisioning a Sustainable Society* (New York: SUNY Press, 1989), 5–6.

21. Center for the American Dream, www.newdream.org.

22. Molly Ivins, National Public Radio.

23. Thomas Berry, *The Dream of the Earth* (San Francisco: Sierra Club Books, 1990), 123.

24. Paul Duchene, "The Last Place on Earth," *Oregonian*, 11 April 1998, B1.

25. Lester Milbrath, *Envisioning a Sustainable Society* (New York: SUNY Press, 1989), 3.

26. Daniel Quinn, *Ishmael* (New York: Bantam, 1993), 40.

27. Marcus Borg, *Meeting Jesus Again for the First Time* (San Francisco: HarperSanFrancisco, 1995), 75.

28. Niles Eldredge, *Dominion* (New York: Henry Holt, 1995), 93.

29. Milbrath, 150.

30. Ruth Sivard, *World Military and Social Expenditures 1996* (Washington, D.C.: World Priorities, 1996), 20.

31. Lester Brown, *State of the World 1994* (New York: W. W. Norton, 1994), 141.

32. Michael Dowd, *Earthspirit* (Mystic, Conn.: Twenty-Third Publications, 1992), 94–101.

33. Center for the American Dream.

34. John Emerich Edward Dalberg-Acton, Letter to Mandell Creighton, April 1887.

35. Henry David Thoreau, *Faith in a Seed* (Washington, D.C.: Island Press, 1993).

36. Michael Dowd, *Earthspirit* (Mystic, Conn.: Twenty-Third Publications, 1992), 76.

37. Moira Gunn, "Tech-Nation," National Public Radio.

38. For a more thorough treatment of the concept of "enoughness," I strongly recommend Joe Dominguez and Vicki Robin, *Your Money or Your Life* (New York: Penguin, 1993). Another very good book on the subject of enoughness is the now-classic *Voluntary Simplicity* by Duane Elgin (New York: Quill, 1993).

39. Marcus Borg, *Jesus: A New Vision* (San Francisco: HarperSan-Francisco, 1992), 193.

40. Thomas Cleary, *The Secret of the Golden Flower* (San Francisco: HarperSanFrancisco, 1991), 25.

41. Thich Nhat Hanh, *Being Peace* (Berkeley: Parallax Press, 1988).

42. This oft-cited quote from Thomas Merton has proved difficult to track to its source. Any reader who can fill in the blank is encouraged to contact the author.

43. Michael Dowd, *Earthspirit* (Mystic, Conn.: Twenty-Third Publications, 1992), 76.

44. Quoted in Dowd, 77.

45. Albert Einstein, "What I Believe" (quoted in *Bartlett's Familiar Quotations*).

46. James Lovelock, *The Gaia Hypothesis* (New York: Harmony-Crown, 1991). An interesting book on the subject of planetary self-regulation.

47. Charlotte Joko Beck, *Everyday Zen* (San Francisco: HarperSan-Francisco, 1989), 14.

48. Beck, v.

49. David Ehrenfeld, "The Coming Collapse of the Age of Technology," *Tikkun,* January-February 1999, 33, 71.

50. Ernest Callenbach and Michael Phillips, *A Citizen Legislature* (Berkeley, Calif.: Banyan Tree Books, 1985).

51. R. H. Blyth, *Haiku, Volume One* (Tokyo: Hokuseido Press, 1981).

52. Coleman Barks, *The Essential Rumi* (San Francisco: HarperSan-Francisco, 1995), 32.

53. Alan AtKisson, "The Innovation Diffusion Game," *In Context,* spring 1991, 58.

GLOSSARY

Auto-Totality: A totalitarian state with no one in control.

Breakers: People whose fundamental operating belief is "I am separate," and whose operating assumption is "There is not enough." The Breaker story is "Creating a World That Works for Me." Breakers treat the Earth as their own property, a life support system for them to use as they please. They seek ever greater control over all aspects of life on Earth, while behaving as though they were exempt from the laws of Nature.

Culture: The set of behaviors shared by a group of people. Culture is the external indicator of a shared consciousness.

Exclusivity: Any set of behaviors based on the belief that our lives are separate, that what I do to you has no effect on me, and that all beings exist primarily to be used and controlled for my benefit.

Inclusivity: Any set of behaviors based on the belief that our lives are inextricably linked with each other, so that whatever I do has an effect on you. Inclusivity is the Golden Rule in practice.

Keepers: Indigenous people who live their lives inextricably connected to their local ecology. Their fundamental operating belief is "We are One." Keepers behave as though they are a part of the Earth. For them, no one group or species is more important than any other.

Menders: People whose fundamental operating belief is "We are One," and whose operating assumption is "There is enough for all." Menders seek to restore balance with the Earth, and consciously live their lives as an integral part of a living, sacred planet. They seek ways to bring healing to themselves and to the Earth.

The Mess: The nightmarish complex of societal and personal problems that afflict today's world. The Mess is incapable of being cleaned up with our current techniques of problem solving. The Mess is the polar opposite of the Web of Life.

The Other: A person or group unfamiliar to you. The Other can take on threatening or sinister connotations for those operating from the Breaker "I am separate" consciousness.

Spirit: The Essence, Power, Intelligence, and transcendental System that lies behind all things and is beyond human rationality and control. Awareness of Spirit may arise both inside and outside the context of "religion."

Spiritual starvation: A condition in which inner contact with Spirit and its many expressions is blocked.

Story: The underlying framework of a set of cultural behaviors.

Violence: Any thought, word, or deed that treats a being like an object or diminishes a being's sense of value or security.

Web of Life: The totality of life on Earth, seen in all its interconnectedness. The Web is a self-regulating, self-evolving system of interlocking subsystems.

THE AUTHOR

SHARIF ABDULLAH is a leading proponent and catalyst for inclusive social, cultural, and spiritual transformation. He is founder and current president of Commonway Institute, dedicated to the creation of a society reflecting our deepest spiritual values. Initially funded by the Rockefeller Foundation, the institute is designed to build inclusivity, understanding, and civic engagement among diverse groups.

Sharif's early life, in Camden, New Jersey, was a study in toxic relationships, including welfare, public housing, grinding poverty, almost constant violence, and a polluted environment. In the mid-Sixties, he was a founder of the Black People's Unity Movement, which promoted self-help and development in Camden's inner city.

He received a B.A. in psychology from Clark University in Massachusetts and a juris doctor degree from Boston University. He then spent six years as a practicing attorney in North Carolina, representing a broad range of clients, from indigent families to businesspeople seeking new ways to serve their communities. For his innovative self-help and community empowerment activities, he received the first of several national awards.

Despite professional success, Sharif became increasingly disillusioned with the adversarial process as a means of achieving inclusive community. He decided to give up his practice and devote himself to a path of social change that was positive and inclusive, honoring the dignity of all beings.

Sharif has worked with thousands of individuals and facilitated scores of transformation, empowerment, and leadership sessions for various public and private clients, including city and county governments, federal agencies, the United Nations, major corporations, and organizations in the fields of personal growth and global transformation.

He has taught the principles of inclusivity at Marylhurst University in Portland, Oregon, and at the University of California at Berkeley.

Sharif is the author of *The Power of One: Authentic Leadership in Turbulent Times*. In addition, he has published many articles on values, personal and cultural transformation, and empowerment.

He has served as chair of the Charlotte–Mecklenburg Minority Affairs Commission in North Carolina and the Portland Affordable Rental Housing Commission. He has also been a board member for the Federal Home Loan Bank Housing Advisory Board and the Association for Humanistic Psychology. He is currently on the board of the Positive Futures Network, which publishes *YES! A Journal of Positive Futures*.

Sharif's international work for inclusivity has taken him to seventeen countries on five continents. In 1998, at the invitation of President Václav Havel of the Czech Republic, Sharif participated as a delegate to the Forum 2000 conference in Prague.

INDEX